HIDDEN HISTORY *of* SPANISH NEW MEXICO

HIDDEN HISTORY *of* SPANISH NEW MEXICO

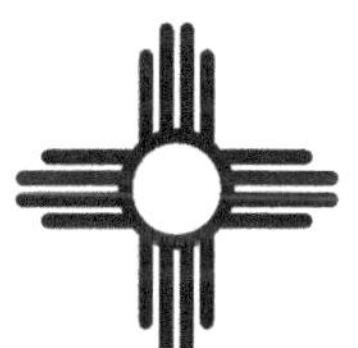

Ray John de Aragón

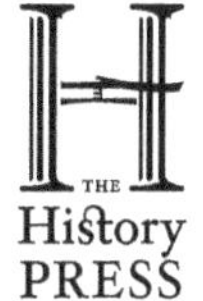

Published by The History Press
Charleston, SC 29403
www.historypress.net

First published 2012

Manufactured in the United States

ISBN 978.1.60949.760.6

Library of Congress CIP data applied for.

Notice: The information in this book is true and complete to the best of our knowledge. It is offered without guarantee on the part of the author or The History Press. The author and The History Press disclaim all liability in connection with the use of this book.

En Memoria—In Memoriam
Juana de Aragón
1649–1680
Killed at Taos during the Pueblo Indian Uprising

I dedicate this book to our ancestors, the Spanish colonists in New Mexico who went through hardships; died from attack, thirst, hunger and disease; and felt the deep pain of losing loved ones they had to bury on sacred ground. This hidden history needs to be brought to the surface and put into its rightful place on the American record of achievement. Hopefully this book will help with this. I dedicate this book to that effort and to Lucía Dolores de Aragón and Linda Dulcinea Isabella de Aragón, who lost their lives at a young age but whom Mie Shu Ou, a dear friend and recognized painter, called, "The heart, spirit and soul of Nuevo México."

Contents

Contents

Introduction

In New Mexico, the Spanish settlers formed a vibrant and distinct Hispano culture that today displays a strength gained over four hundred years of settlement. This pride is shown in music, visual art and literature. Contrary to what has been written, New Mexico was not totally isolated from the outside world. When goods and supplies were brought into New Mexico, the colonists had access to literature, such as the novel *Lazarillo de Tormes*, one of the world's foremost novels by an unknown author, published in 1554; and the work of Félix Lope de Vega Carpio, the most prolific Spanish dramatist, who wrote over 1,800 plays. By the 1800s, New Mexico authors were getting their books published, among them *Ojeada sobre Nuevo México* (*A Glimpse of New Mexico*), written by Antonio Barreiro. Manuel Salazar wrote the first groundbreaking novel in New Mexico, titled *La Historia de un Caminante o Sea, Gervacio y Aurora* (*The History of a Traveler, or Gervacio and Aurora*), and Eusebio Chacón published two novels, *El Hijo de la Tempestad* (*Son of the Tempest*) and *Tras la Tormenta la Calma* (*The Calm After the Storm*).

A Spanish history of New Mexico would not be complete without mention that from before the mid-nineteenth century and up to the twenty-first century, Spanish and bilingual (Spanish-English) newspapers have been published. Almost every single rural village had a printing press. Newspapers such as *El Nuevo Mexicano* (the *New Mexican*), *La Verdad* (the *Truth*; 1845), *La Estrella* (Mora, New Mexico), *La Gaceta* (circa 1850), *La Flecha* (Wagon Mound), *La Cronica del Río Colorado* (the *Red River Chronicle*; Red River, 1880), *El Farol, El Unico Periódico Castellano al sur de Las Vegas y al Oriente de el*

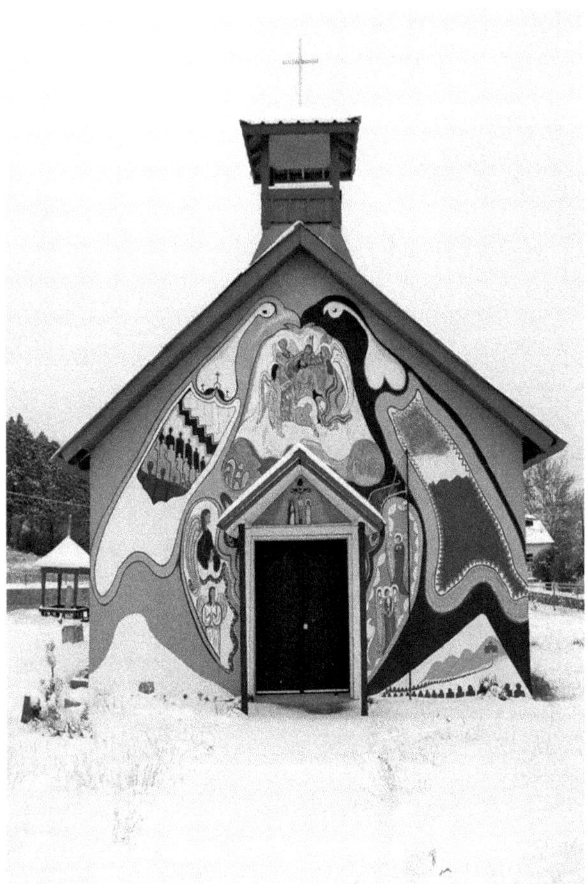

La Capilla, Las Vegas, New Mexico. *Photograph ©Ramón Juan Carlos de Aragón, 2011.*

Río Grande (the *Lantern, the only Castilian Newspaper South of Las Vegas and East of the Rio Grande*), *El Payo de Nuevo Méjico* (1845; *payo* in reference to being native) and *La Voz del Pueblo* (Las Vegas, New Mexico; 1892). The associate editor for *La Voz del Pueblo* was Ezequiel C. de Baca, born in Las Vegas in 1864. He became New Mexico's first lieutenant governor in 1912. At any given time, over 250 Spanish-language newspapers were being published in New Mexico. This prompted the establishment of the Hispanic American Press Association in New Mexico. Spanish-language publishing houses such as El Nuevo Mexicano in Santa Fé, La Revista Catolica and the Spanish American Publishing Company in Las Vegas complemented the work of the newspapers by putting out books, pamphlets and other printed materials such as broadsides. The well-known Spanish Sociedad Literaria (Literary Society) met with a renowned group of native Hispano authors for over two decades, starting in 1881 in Las Vegas. In 1884, José Segura founded *El Boletín Popular* (the *Popular Bulletin*), a newspaper that highlighted the arts and writers in New Mexico. Segura published two novellas by Eusebio Chacón.

In the mid-1800s, Doña Barbara Chávez de Sánchez, the niece of general and governor Don Manuel Armijo, owned novels by Victor Hugo. She motivated and inspired her grandson, U.S. senator Dionisio (Dennis) Chávez. Aurora Lucero preserved New Mexico Hispano culture through her writings. Fabiola Cabeza de Baca's book, *We Fed Them Cactus*, detailing Spanish life and folkways in New Mexico, was a bestseller.

Spanish music and dances from the different provinces of Spain formed the basis for the diverse, yet similar, traditional folk music and dance styles that developed in the Spanish Americas, which are now called folkloric dance and music. For example, New Mexican dance incorporated the Scottish round dance, polkas from Poland, French waltzes and traditional dances from Spain. Lucía de Aragón (1892–1938), born in Las Vegas, New Mexico, was a professional ballet dancer in New York City during the 1920s. She owned the New Mexico Salt Refining Company near Willard. Rosalía de Aragón, stage and film actor and singer of popular New Mexican music, continues the tradition of the indomitable spirit of New Mexican Spanish women. Cleofas Martínez de Jaramillo founded the well-known Sociedad Folklórica in Santa Fé to promote and preserve New Mexico Spanish culture, and J.M. Hilario Alaríd, who is recognized as a writer of ballads, organized La Banda Lírica, a twenty-five-piece orchestra that played traditional and original New Mexican compositions.

The presentation of dramatic performances in the villages was also significant, with plays like *Los Moros y Cristianos*, which portrayed the defeat of the Moors by the Christians. Rosa María Calles, visual artist (Santera), playwright, producer and director, broke records with her musical stage production *Cuento de La Llorona* (*Tale of the Wailing Woman*), based on New Mexico's Spanish colonial history. These historical and artistic admixtures have developed a rich and vibrant Hispanic heritage in the beautiful state of New Mexico.

In 1884, the legendary Elfego Baca fought the famous Wild West gun battle at Frisco, New Mexico, against eighty rowdy Texas cowboys who had been shooting up the peaceful San Francisco village. Baca went on to become a noted western lawman and was immortalized in the film *The Nine Lives of Elfego Baca*, produced by Disney Studios. In 1892, Felix Martínez was recognized as the founder of what would become New Mexico Highlands University.

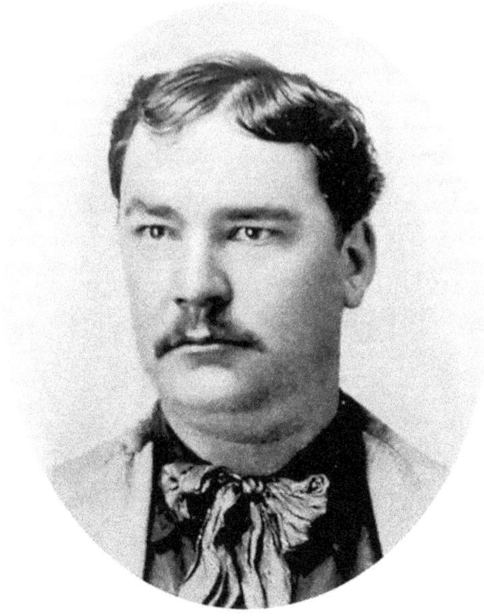

Elfego Baca. Photographer unknown. *Courtesy of the author.*

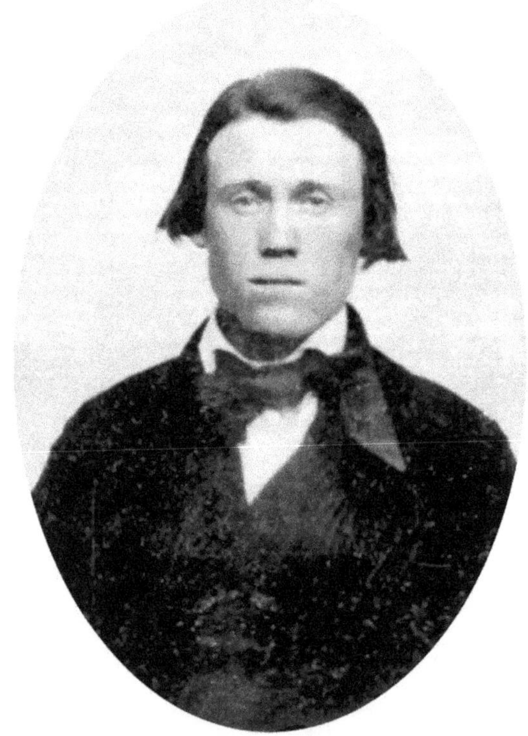

Manuel Antonio Chávez. Ambrotype, mid-nineteenth century. *Courtesy of the author.*

During the Territorial Period, Hispanic New Mexicans distinguished themselves in all walks of life, including in the U.S. military. At the time of the Civil War, Hispanics composed approximately 90 percent of the New Mexico Union volunteers, including cavalry, infantry and officers. The most famous was Colonel Manuel Antonio Chávez, "El Leoncito" (the Little Lion), who helped defeat the Confederates as the hero of the Battle of Glorieta. In all, New Mexico Hispanic Union volunteers defeated the Confederates in three battles and forced them out of New Mexico after they had taken over the capitol in Santa Fé. New Mexican Hispanic troops were also recognized for their bravery as Teddy Roosevelt's Rough Riders during the Spanish-American War. However, Bishop Jean-Baptiste Lamy's arrival in 1851 and America's entry into World War I and, especially, World War II would dramatically and adversely affect the Spanish history of New Mexico with far-reaching consequences.

Miguel de Cervantes, who is considered by many to be one of the greatest writers in the history of the world and who wrote the famous book *Don Quixote de la Mancha* in 1610, said, "We are children of our deeds." This is reflected in our history, our traditions, our heritage our culture and our language. This pride is shown in our music, visual art and literature, as in the following poetic composition in honor of the descendants of the Spanish colonizers, written by Juan del Valle in Española, New Mexico, in October 1931:

Ode to the Hispano People

Descendant of the race of Titans,
Suffered, religious and faithful Hispano,
People of a noble soul and of healthful body
Raised well with proverbs and strict gestures.

Your body well formed and robust,
Slender like the pine trees of your mountains,
Made strong with your eternal wars with races,
And, by your sullen work.

The color of your complexion, white and smooth,
Like your beautiful daughters of Castile,
You know you are the envy of your sisters,
The ermine, the silk, and the fowl.

The color of your complexion,
The color of iron, furrowed with wrinkles,
That finished the insomnia,
The tortures your parents endured
With the fierce people.

The light of life that shines in your eyes,
Has the darkness of the ocean,
And the brilliance of Hispano genius,
And the scars of the sky of Castile.

May you ever be praised proud native people,
That speaks the sweet language of Spain,
And adding to your glory new deeds,
With English that you master my friend.

May you ever be praised oh native Hispano people,
Full of pride for your God and your Saints,
In your face and your pious temples
Hospitable and grand Samaritan.

Hear me, why in your glories you have fallen asleep?
And have allowed your heritage to be taken?
Wake up people of mine, and take flight
As you take back the glories you've lost.

Be lazy no more, and rest no longer,
It is time to move and be noticed,
And lift our sacred people
Into a secure and lofty place.

To show pride and humility is not shameful,
To seek justice is our right,
Let us come together in battle
Forgetting and forgiving our differences.

This poem graphically illustrates the indomitable spirit of the Hispanic ancestors of New Mexico who were proud of their history, traditions and culture. It is also reminiscent of the *corrido* ballads that most often honor heroic people and deeds. The popularity of poetic writings in New Mexico was enormous.

The Spanish Empire was global, and the influence of Spanish culture was so pervasive, especially in the Americas, that Spanish is still the native tongue of more than 200 million people outside Spain. The language itself is the unifying force. Spanish, for example, is the third most spoken language in the world, after Chinese and English. The Spanish spoken is actually Castellano, the language of Castilla, which was the kingdom of Queen Isabella.

Although the Spanish language developed over centuries, as did the Spanish character, and many civilizations had an impact on this development, what defines an individual of Spanish origin is the culture itself. The local Spanish of an area may contain regionalisms—words that identify things or have meanings that are distinct to the region and are not common to the overall language. That is why the Spanish spoken in Mexico may be somewhat different from that spoken in Ecuador, Cuba, Spain, Puerto Rico and New Mexico.

A journey back in time shows the development of today's Spanish language and its major influences. Spanish got the words *vega* (meadow) and *izquierdo* (left) from the Iberians, as well as the names Javier and Elvira. Some of the words the Spanish language took from the Greeks are *escuela* (school), *yeso* (gesso), *quemar* (to burn), *huérfano* (orphan), *golpe* (hit), *gobernar* (to govern), *botica* (drugstore), *cuerda* (cord) and the name Estevan. Castellano itself was derived from Latin, the language spoken by the Romans. This can be clearly seen in words like *legenda* in Latin and *leyenda* in Spanish, *dolorosa* in Latin and the same in Spanish, *lacrimas* in Latin and *lagrimas* in Spanish, *tristes* in Latin and *triste* in Spanish, *quando* in Latin and *cuando* in Spanish, *Gloria* in Latin and the same in Spanish, et cetera. The Visigoths contributed words like *espuelos* (spurs), *estribo* (stirrup) and *heraldo* (herald). The Moors introduced *alabado* (praised), *arroz* (rice), *algodón* (cotton), *zanahoria* (carrot), *acequia* (ditch), *noria* (well), *alcalde* (mayor) and many others. Other languages enriched and continue to enrich the Spanish language. For example, from the French, the language gets *chaqueta* (jacket), *pantalónes* (pants or trousers), *jardín* (garden) and *tejer* (to sew). From Italian, Spanish incorporated *diseño* (design), *novela* (novel), *soneto* (sonnet) and *charlar* (to talk). Native Americans contributed *maíz* (corn), *sabana* (sheet), *tomate* (tomato), *papa* (potato), *canoa* (canoe) and *huracán* (hurricane). There has also been a tremendous assimilation of Spanish words into the English language, beginning with the opening of the Santa Fé Trail in New Mexico around 1822. Hispano New Mexicans passed on many words to the Americans entering the territory that became part of

English vocabulary, such as *arroyo*, *patio*, *rodeo*, *bronco*, *canyon*, *corral*, *palomino*, *pinto*, *coyote*, *chaparral*, *adobe*, *mesa*, et cetera.

The twentieth century ushered in a vast number of new ideas, discoveries and approaches to New Mexico. Young Hispanic men went off to foreign wars and saw new things. They returned home and brought changes, which made New Mexico more global in its outlook. These changes affected the formerly agrarian culture, especially after World Wars I and II. New Mexico Hispanics continued their deep involvement in government and issues that affected the entire country and the world.

Many different cultures have enriched Hispanic history, with roots in the Iberian Peninsula from 1700 BC to AD 1492. The Spanish arrived in the Southwest with Alvar Nuñez Cabeza de Vaca in AD 1535, nearly one hundred years before the pilgrims landed at Plymouth Rock. Francis Borgia Steck wrote:

> *Historical articles in the United States have an absence of information especially between the late 16th and mid 18th century, particularly about the contributions of the Spanish and the Patronato Real. Some historians have even condemned, as a whole, the Spanish enterprise in America...It is not often that a school history of the United States fails to describe the inhumanity of the Spaniards. These histories often fail to give credit to many Spanish missionaries, bishops, and at times governors, who denounced the abuse of the natives, sought their protection, and introduced important spiritual and cultural contributions to the Indian cultures. A review of these publications indicates that the early history in the United States is almost entirely limited to the history of the European immigrants who settled in the Eastern coast of North America. Historians have been biased against Spanish heritage in America.*

Many roots created the one tree we call Hispanic, with branches that spread throughout the world. Understanding these roots and branches, and having a deeper insight into Hispanos in New Mexico and their place in a history that is mostly concealed, is what this book is about.

Historical Genesis of New Mexico Hispanics

Birth of an Empire

No culture stands on its own; rather, it builds on or disrupts what came before and gives birth to a new way of seeing, expressing and experiencing life. Tradition is the outcome, and it is unique to each community, even if the recipe is the same. Who can say when the first seed was planted? Many different cultures have enriched New Mexico's Hispanic history since ancient times, from the Old World to the New World.

Who came first to the Iberian Peninsula, the motherland? Los Vascones, Basques, Los Vascos (as the Romans called a distinct ethnic group that appeared in the western Pyrenees), or was it the Iberians? Some say it was the Basques, who spoke a pre-Indo-European language. However, with technological advancement and improved archaeological dating of artifacts, it now appears that it might have been the Iberians. Marcelino Sanz de Sautuola discovered some Iberian caves in 1879. In these caves were artifacts such as the double-edged stone hand axes from over one million years ago and elaborate cave paintings. The Altamira Cave paintings in Northern Spain of bison and other animals by the Magdalenian people have been in existence for more than eleven thousand years and far exceed the skill of other cave paintings due to the number of colors, perspective and lighting used. But whoever came first, it was only the beginning of the evolution of a proud people.

Cerdos Ibericos, La Matanza and Hispanic New Mexico's Diet

The origin of the *matanza* goes back to early Spain. The Iberians, more than likely, were the first on the peninsula to have a community festival to slaughter an animal and cook it for all to enjoy. The animal might have been a wild boar, but in time it became a lamb, cow or domesticated pig. *Cerdos Ibericos*, Iberian pigs, were domesticated as early as 7000 BC, and pork was so ingrained in the Iberian diet that it became synonymous with Iberian identity. After the Iberians converted to Christianity, the eating of pork set them apart from Arabs and Jews, who were forbidden by their religions from eating the meat of pigs.

With the colonization of the New World, the Spanish brought with them the ancient tradition of the matanza from Castile, Spain. Of course, there were no refrigerators or freezers, so meat was not frozen, and pork was never used for jerky. By having the matanzas scheduled at different times from house to house during the winter months between December and March, when the cold days keep bacteria levels at their lowest, it was ensured that everyone would have a continuous supply of fresh meat. Donald Chávez y Gilbert, who knows the tradition in New Mexico, describes a typical matanza in *La Matanza: A Hispanic Tradition*:

> *Each Matanza was an event sometimes two years in the making, as two years is about the period needed for hogs to reach optimal weight. Family members were trained and delegated responsibilities based on their age and station in the family unit, beginning with daily feeding all the way up to the expert bleeding and butcher skills needed the day of the killing (matanza). Generally, the older men consisted of the killing crew and butchering large cuts of meat. The women prepared the many other aspects of cooking as if they did it day in and day out, cutting carnitas (thin-cut pieces of meat), chicharones (deep-fried fat), chopping potatoes and onions, cooking beans, chile, posole (hominy), tortillas…the day before La Matanza water was hauled in buckets from a hand drilled well or nearby acequia (irrigation ditch), to fill fifty gallon drums. The drums were placed over a pit where a large enough fire could be ignited to bring the barrels of water to a boil…Depending on your specific role or responsibility determined when you arrived. When I was an adolescent, I was old enough to take responsibility for keeping the water barrels full and boiling and ensuring a flow of hot water buckets to the men scraping off the hair…I was not seasoned enough to do the bleeding or butchering. I would*

> *have to get my practice beginning with cutting strips of lonja (fat)...A little before daybreak the fire was started and while the water was heated to a boil, the hog was brought to the butcher site only a few feet away from the fire. Our family used a slatted wood table not too far from the fire, the table elevated above a hole in the ground or pit excavated such that unwanted parts and blood could easily drain and collect without getting under foot. The second wave or the killing crew arrived at dawn and killed the hog...it was a sad yet righteous moment when I believe we all silently paid homage to the hog for her sacrifice...and the meaning of the whole Matanza ritual in our long Hispanic roots.*

In the diet of every New Mexican family, and an ingredient in many New Mexican dishes, is chile, both red and green. Chiles were cultivated in the Americas as many as eight thousand years ago. Another important staple is the potato. According to Dr. Hector Flores, professor of plant pathology and biotechnology at Pennsylvania State University, "the most likely origin of the potato is in southern Peru and northeastern Bolivia more than 13,000 years ago. The Conquistadores from Spain first introduced the potato to Europe in 1570. Many Europeans believed the potato was a creation of witches, but eventually it became the most important food for the poor." The delicious meat of pork complemented pots of beans, *chicos*, red and green chile and other delicacies. In the past, pig bristles were used by *santeros* for bristle brushes to create their artwork. Boot makers also used the bristles, and pigskins were used during the colonial era for bookbinding and as writing surfaces for documents.

The Horrid and Belligerent Province

Around 1700 BC, the Greeks gave the name Iberia to the peninsula and called the tribes they found Iberians. The Phoenicians then called the Iberian Peninsula *Hispalis* and the people *Hispani* around 1200 BC. The Iberian Peninsula was known as *Horrida et Bellicosa Provincia*, the "Horrid and Belligerent Province," by the Romans. This birthplace of Hispanic culture, which sits on a body of land surrounded on three sides by water at the tip of the Mediterranean Sea, has a history filled with the stuff of legend, mystery, intrigue and romance. The history has an impact on all those with Hispanic roots in New Mexico and all Spanish-speaking people around the world today.

The Iberians, who were geographically isolated from one another, were divided into separate tribes, with chieftains at the head who directed their daily lives and led them in battle. Each tribe developed a distinct regional and political identity, and they constantly quarreled and fought against one another. But they were also fierce fighters against invaders. In fact, the Phoenicians, Greeks, Carthaginians and Romans all in turn discovered that the Iberians would rather die than be vanquished. Civilizations attempting to conquer Iberia were absorbed into and became part of Iberian culture. The Iberians not only gained in strength, but they also took on the best of Celtic, Phoenician and Carthaginian ways of life and ideas. By the time the Romans attempted to conquer Iberia, the inhabitants were ready for the mightiest army in the world.

During the ninth and seventh centuries BC, the Celts crossed the Pyrenees into Iberia and settled along the Río Ebro and Río Duero. They were farmers and herders who also excelled in metalworking crafts. The community raised the children, and the community owned the land. The Celtic women were tall and very beautiful. They arranged their hair in elaborate braids and wore dyed, embroidered dresses. The Celtic men were also tall and had rippling muscles, white complexions, spiked blond hair and faces and arms tattooed in blue. They loved to fight, sometimes fully naked and with their skin entirely dyed blue. The Celts intermarried with the Iberians, and their offspring were called the Celtiberians. The Celtiberians were influenced more by Celtic culture and common language than by race. The Celtiberian women were equal to men and could own property, which was not the practice in other cultures of their time. The women were strong and courageous and served as ambassadors to avoid war, but if war was inevitable, they were leaders in battle and had the right to kingship. These were the people the Phoenicians met on the Iberian Peninsula.

THE DIFFERENT FACES OF THE IBERIAN PENINSULA

The Phoenicians were an ancient people who occupied Phoenicia on the northern African coast. They founded the prosperous city of Carthage. The commercial empire made its fortune through trade and expanded its domain in the peninsula, where it established thriving trading ports. Phoenician men were hardy and active seamen, as well as avid hunters and skilled ship builders. Phoenicians also became excellent navigators by using the stars at night to guide them. They shipped Iberian Peninsular food, fish, salt, minerals and pottery back to people in their own homeland. They introduced grapevines and olive trees to Iberia. The women were noted for the jewelry they wore from head to foot. Many necklaces, armlets, bracelets, lockets, earrings, fingerings, ornaments for the hair, buckles, buttons and brooches are found at Phoenician excavation sites. During pre-Christian times, Phoenician influence spread throughout the eastern Mediterranean. However, they are most famous for developing the alphabet we use in the world today. These new skills would prove to be important to the Iberians.

The Carthaginians, led by Hamilcar Barca, took control of the Iberian Peninsula in 237 BC. Barca married an Iberian woman, and they had a son whom they called Hannibal. The Carthaginians employed the Celtiberians as mercenary soldiers to help them protect the land. The Greeks had freely moved in and out of the peninsula as early as 3000 BC, and their colony at Massilia, in what is now Catalonia, also maintained commercial ties with the Celtiberians. The Greeks, Carthaginians and Romans were in constant battle in other parts of the western world. Hannibal is famous in western history for leading a Carthaginian army, along with soldiers mounted on elephants, across the Pyrenees to attack Rome. The Romans defeated the Carthaginians in two major wars, and Carthage was totally vanquished by 206 BC, but Carthaginian culture intermingled widely with that of the Iberians, and they coexisted. The Greeks decided to make a greater imprint on the Iberian Peninsula.

The impact of Greek culture in Iberia was through sculpture and trading. The surname Griego, which is found in Hispanic culture throughout the Spanish-speaking world and translates to Greek, is a lasting legacy. One of the most famous artist's in Spanish history, El Greco, is another part of this legacy. Greek activity was mainly commercial, and they were not necessarily interested in colonization. But when their commercial activities were threatened by Roman control, the Greeks placed a greater interest in their presence on the peninsula. By 146 BC, Greek rule had ended and Roman rule had begun.

The Land of the Brutes: Hispania

The Romans sent their best generals and most powerful armies to take over the land of "brutes," as they called the Iberians. The divided tribes were a significant problem for the Roman soldiers, but when Viriatus, an Iberian leader, united the warring factions into one force, they fought with a bravery that impressed even the greatest of generals.

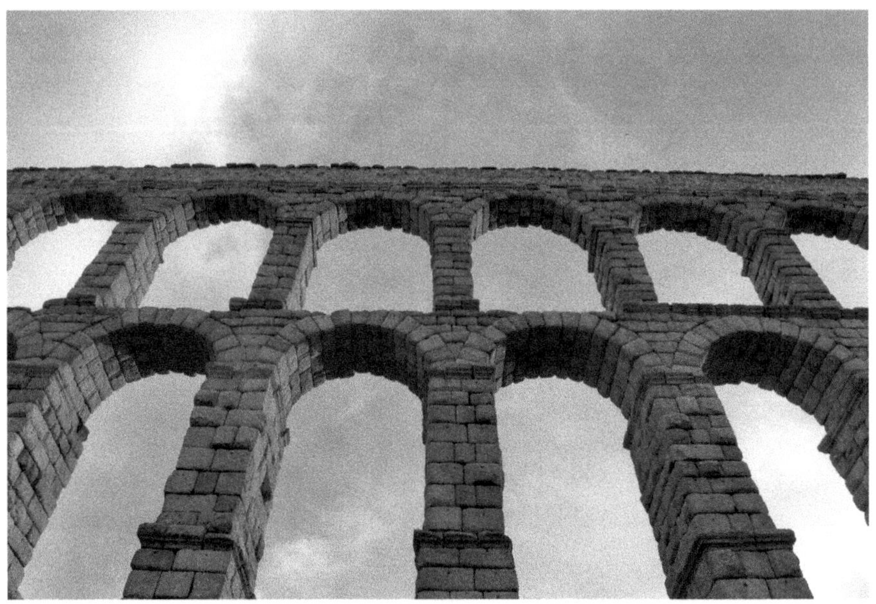

A Roman aqueduct in Segovia. *Photograph ©Ramón Juan Carlos de Aragón, 2011.*

As previously mentioned, the Romans called the Iberian Peninsula Hispania and the people Hispanos. When the Romans intermarried with the Iberians, they referred to the offspring as Hispano-Romans. It was always the role of Roman women to teach their children about Roman culture. Young Roman girls were educated along with the boys, and it was felt to be important to pass on the culture to future generations. This was ingrained in Hispano-Roman society and would continue after the birth of Spain. In time, the Hispano-Romans rose up to such an extent that they controlled Rome and dominated its society as emperors, political leaders, writers and philosophers. Many names recognized in Roman history—such as the Emperors Trajan, Hadrian and Marcus Aurelius, plus the great writer Seneca the Younger—were all Hispano-Romans. Roman influence in Iberia was further felt with the erection of aqueducts and the founding of what would become the major Spanish cities of Valencia, Zaragoza and Mérida. Methods of irrigation and agricultural techniques introduced by the Romans into the Iberian Peninsula are still in use today. Roman arts were integrated into the Iberian arts and developed into what we call traditional Hispano art.

Roman civilization was finally brought down by barbaric Germanic tribes, which included the Franks, Angles, Saxons, Jutes, Goths and Visigoths. Rome had controlled the Western world for over one thousand years, and its influence had been felt everywhere. The decline and fall of the empire was due somewhat to excesses in alcohol addiction, laziness, gambling, obesity, corruption in government and immorality.

Interestingly, when the Romans celebrated, they feasted for days. Needless to say, the health of the Romans, including the soldiers, spiraled downward. The barbaric tribes saw these weaknesses, and they found the time ripe for attack.

The Visigoth Kings

In AD 268, the Visigoths, a Germanic tribe, invaded the Roman Empire and swarmed over the Balkan Peninsula. The western Roman emperor, Honorius, sent his sister, Galla Placidia, and her husband, Ataulf, to restore order to the Iberian Peninsula. Ataulf was a Visigoth king. In return for defending the land, they could settle and govern the inhabitants. By AD 500, the Visigoths were the dominant power on the Iberian Peninsula; they set up kingdoms and built fortified castles throughout the land. Toledo was established as the capital, and also established was the reign of successive Visigothic kings. The Visigoth king permitted marriages between his people and the local Hispanos. Most of the nobility converted to Islam. In 589, the

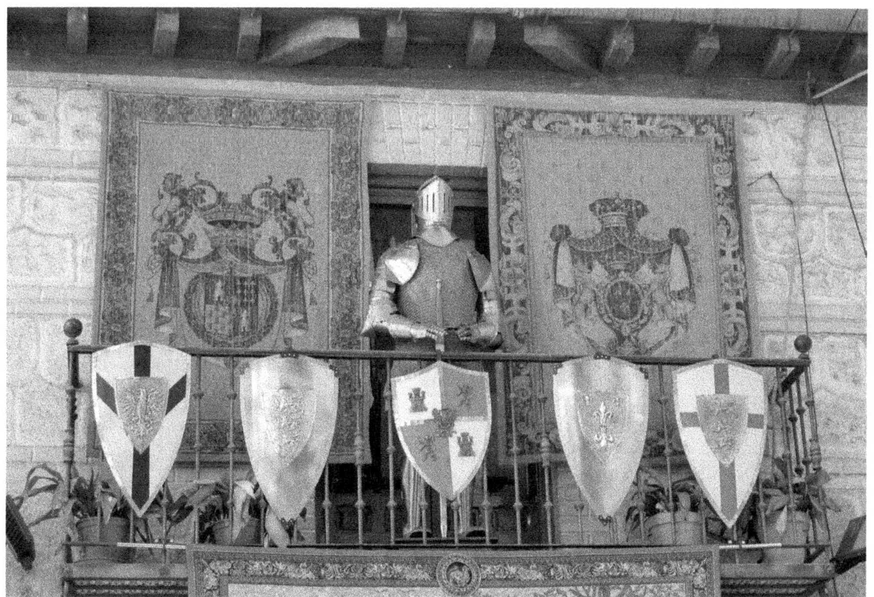

Toledo, Spain. *Photograph ©Ramón Juan Carlos de Aragón, 2011.*

Visigoth ruler Recared converted to Catholicism. Under the Romans, the prominent role of the mother was to teach her children about their culture and faith. This shifted with the Visigoths. Under the Visigoths, formal education and government were the responsibilities of the church. Still, civil war, royal assassinations and usurpation were commonplace, which led to another form of foreign intervention in the peninsula. In 711, a group of Arabs and Berbers, also known in history as the Moors, invaded Hispania and brought most of the country under Islamic control.

Andalucía and the Alhambra

Theatrical plays and historical drama led to the intrigue of the capture of the Iberian Peninsula by the Moors. The legend, myth or truth revolves around King Rodrigo (d. 711) and a nobleman, Count Julian. Julian sent his

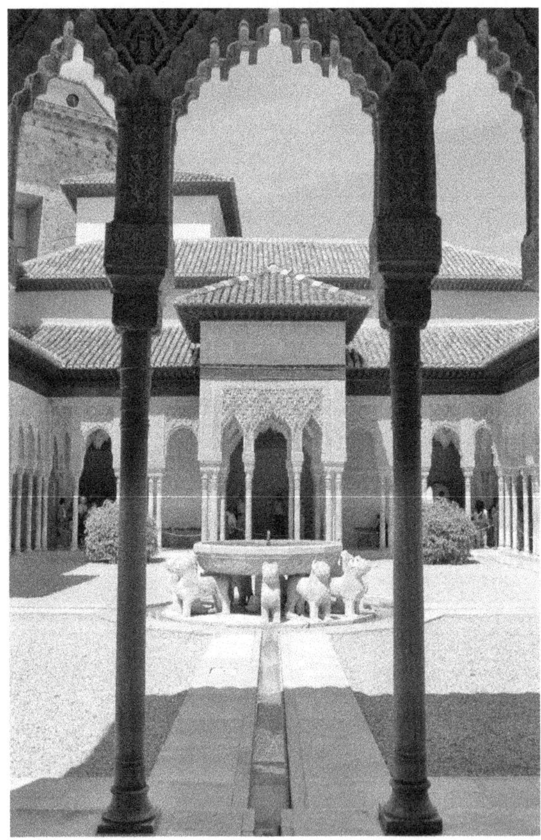

Alhambra. *Photograph ©Ramón Juan Carlos de Aragón, 2011.*

daughter to be educated under the protection of King Rodrigo. The king and the nobleman's daughter fell in love, and they married against the wishes of her father. To defend his honor and avenge his king, Julian plotted against his country by allowing the takeover of the peninsula by Emir (Governor) Musa ibn Nusayr, the Muslim ruler of North Africa. The Arabs had been eyeing the land across the Mediterranean, and now with the help of Julian, they could cross the legendary protected Pillars of Hercules, which would guarantee success.

The Caliph al-Walid accepted Count Julian's invitation to cross onto the peninsula under the condition that he convert to Islam. The count tricked King Rodrigo into believing that he was gathering soldiers to fight the Arabs, who were planning to cross Jebel-ut-Tarik, or Gibraltar. They arrived at the battle site, but Count Julian had convinced the soldiers to turn against King Rodrigo. King Rodrigo realized he had been led into a trap. He escaped but drowned on his return to his castle. Count Julian spent the rest of his life in misery and unhappiness, knowing he had betrayed his people, who spent the next seven hundred years in battle trying to oust the invaders.

At the same time, Islamic territories, which were called al-Andalus (Andalucía) under the Muslims, flourished because the residents in these areas lived in harmony with the Christians and Jews. Hispano-Islamic art, literature, science and architecture developed during this period. The Moors built beautiful palaces, public baths, schools and gardens. The capital city of Córdoba in al-Andalus became one of the greatest intellectual centers of Europe because of its schools and libraries. The Kingdom of Toledo was ruled over by a caliph and had a sumptuous palace known as the Alhambra.

Reconquista

A document written during AD 800 is the first to refer to the land protected by castles as Castilla. The first count of Castilla was Rodrigo, in 850, who fought alongside his king, Alfonso I, during the Reconquista. The Reconquista was not just about military victory on the Iberian Peninsula by Christian rulers against the Moors but also about the type of warrior people who would defend its borders and make it their home.

Castilla began as a buffer for the Kingdom of León along the upper Río Ebro. The warriors who settled the region were free peasants who were granted independence, special privileges and immunities by the kings of León in exchange for defending the frontier through the hardships and isolation of

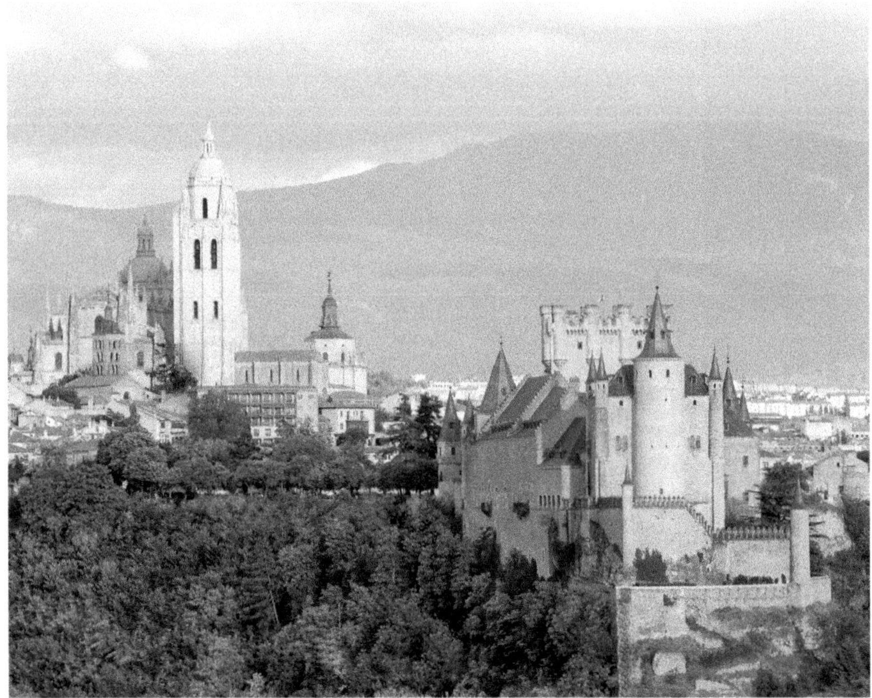

Segovia Cathedral and Castle. *Photograph ©Ramón Juan Carlos de Aragón, 2011.*

the region. Castilla developed its own dialect, values, traditions and culture, which were fashioned by the tough conditions. Castilian men and women fought alongside one another against the enemy. They believed and lived in a society in which a person's reputation and honor was to be protected. The period of the reconquest of the Iberian Peninsula took roughly eight hundred years, from AD 718 to January 2, 1492. Christians from all over Europe felt it was their Christian duty to do penance and volunteer to help in the fight to restore Castilla back to its Christian rule.

The apostle Saint James the Greater (*Santé Iago*, "Saint James" in Spanish) introduced the Christian faith in the first century AD to the Iberian Peninsula. During the long struggle to drive the Muslims from the Iberian Peninsula, the bones of Saint James were discovered, and a great cathedral was built on the site where his remains were found. They called the cathedral Santiago de Compostela. Kings, queens, Christian soldiers and thousands of pilgrims journeyed there since miracles were attributed to the site. The Holy Shroud (burial cloth of Jesus) reappeared after years of being lost. The Holy House (the house where Mary, the mother of Jesus had lived) was recognized by the pope sixteen years after its translocation. The miraculous statue of Our Lady of Guadalupe, which disappeared in AD 711 during the Moorish invasion, reappeared in Montserrat, near Barcelona, after six hundred years. Holy people who were recognized by Christians and Moors alike—such as Saint Francis of Assisi, Saint Anthony of Padua, Saint Therese of Avila, Saint Catherine of Siena, et cetera—lived during the Reconquista. Miracles, appearances of saints and martyrdoms were commonplace, and it inspired the people to fight to the death if that's what it took to restore God's kingdom on earth.

Another Spanish epic marvel was an eleventh-century knight whom they called El Cid.

The Legend of El Cid

When we look back in history, we find some men and women who are recognized for bravery, honor and the courage to stand up for a cause they feel is right or just. This is the legend of one of those men. It began when

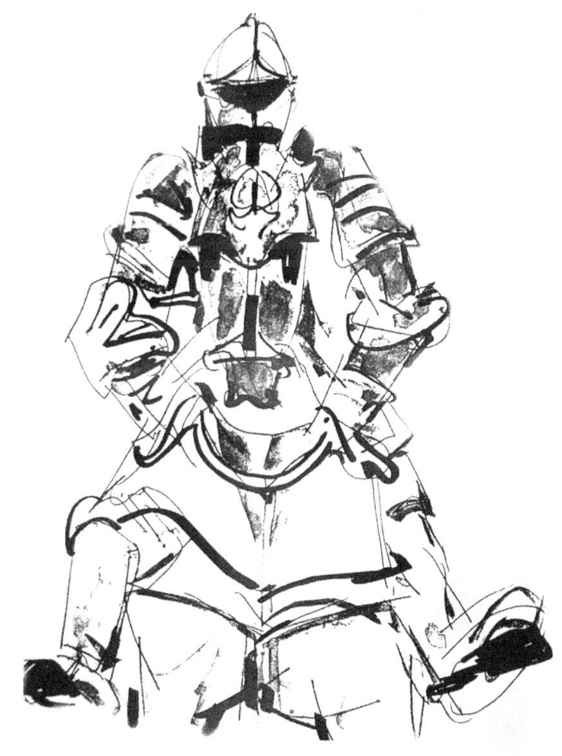

Conquistador, Mie Shu Ou, 1985. Pen-and-ink drawing. *Courtesy of the author.*

Christians circulated stories that the spirit of Saint James had actually appeared riding on a white horse and waving a sword as he led them into battle. Stories of his appearance spread, and soon the Iberians began to shout, "Santiago!" as they fought the Moors, calling for the help of their warrior saint.

A national hero arose: Rodrigo Díaz de Vivar (circa 1043–1099), a military leader who was victorious against the Moors. Rodrigo became the ideal *caballero*, or romanticized horseman-gentleman, because he was extremely dedicated to his faith, his country, his king, his wife and his family. He became such a legend in his own time that the Moors themselves feared and respected him. They called him *Sidi*, which in Arabic means "sir" or "lord." The word was Hispanicized to *El Cid*. The Christian knights called Rodrigo *El Campeador*, the "Champion," so he became known throughout the land as *El Cid Campeador*.

It is said that El Cid never lost a battle. He and his knights wore heavy metal armor when fighting. They all had *escuderos*, or squires, who cared for and polished their armor and weapons. El Cid's sword, which was called *El Tizón*, was thought to have magical powers by the Moors, and his warhorse, Babieca, was also feared. The Christians used colorful banners and standards that represented their kingdoms and the saints to whom they were dedicated. The military order of Santiago was created, and this became the largest and strongest of the knight orders. Surnames also developed to identify where a knight came from.

The Iberian king, Fernando the Great, son of Sancho III of Navarre, was married to Queen Sancha. His followers and family revered him as an "exceedingly strong emperor" who fought gallantly in the Reconquista and took back for the people of Castilla much of the province from the Moors. He became ill during his takeover of Valencia and returned home. The historian Ramón Menéndez Pidal records that he took his fate with many expressions of "ardent piety, having laid aside his crown and royal mantle, dressed in the robe of a monk and lying on a bier covered with ashes, which was placed before the altar of the Basilica of San Isidoro." He divided his kingdom among his three sons: the eldest, Alfonso, received León; Sancho received Castilla; and the third son, García, received a portion of Galicia.

After Fernando's death, Sancho wanted to reunite the kingdom of his father and attacked his brothers with a very young noble, Rodrigo Díaz de Bivar, at his side. El Cid personified the bright, shining, unstoppable leader who struck fear in the hearts of his enemies and made them tremble with the mere sound of his name. He was also the embodiment of chivalry and virtue. Sancho was killed in a battle at Zamora. León, Castilla and Galicia became part of the kingdom of Sancho's brother, Alfonso VI. Alfonso VI exiled Rodrigo from his empire because El Cid suspected Alfonso of Sancho's murder. Alfonso VI was having problems on the battlefield, and he went into exile, fearing his own death. He recalled El Cid to service. El Cid would not fight for him unless he swore in front of Saint Agatha's holy relics that he was not responsible for Sancho's death. Alfonso placed his hand on the relics and swore he wasn't. El Cid again made the king repeat and swear that he was innocent of his brother's murder, which the king did, but he would never trust Alfonso again. Finally, El Campeador agreed to fight in the name of Alfonso to retake Valencia from the Moors. Alfonso made Rodrigo the chief general, and El Cid became Alfonso's most valuable asset.

Rodrigo gained the title Campeador when he fought for Castilla against an Aragónese knight; El Cid won the battle in single combat. Single combat was sometimes used to prevent the greater loss of soldiers' lives on the battlefield. El Cid then gathered soldiers, some of whom were Moors who did not have allegiance to the Muslim cause, and they fought together against the Almoravids. El Cid was victorious and halted the seizure of the Christian kingdoms from the Moors at Valencia.

El Cid remained as the prince of Valencia with his wife, Jimena de Gormaz, a relative of Alfonso. There was peace in Valencia for some time, except for periodic skirmishes. The Almoravids, Muslim militia of fifteen thousand men, came into Valencia with such ferocity that they killed everyone with whom they came into contact. El Cid was able to pursue them and route the Moors toward the river, where many of the Muslims drowned. The Moors who became El Cid's subjects were allowed to remain in Valencia at peace and to worship their god in their mosques. El Cid later became ill and physically weak. He could no longer lead his men. He would send out armies, but at times few returned. Some say he died from sorrow after the death of his son, Diego Rodríguez, when he did not return from one of these battles.

A legend of El Cid has survived and is told by writer Thomas Pluck. It says that on his deathbed, El Cid received a vision from the apostle Saint Peter that a great victory against the Moors would come after his death. When the Almoravids took siege of Valencia, his wife, Jimena, had his men mount the dead body of El Cid on his favorite warhorse, Babieca, with his sword, Tizón, in the middle of the night. In the morning, the knights made a surprise attack. The Moorish king awoke, and it seemed to him that there appeared seventy thousand knights all dressed in robes as white as snow, led by El Cid carrying a snow-white banner in one hand and, in the other, a sword that shone as if on fire. The Moors tried to escape to their ships, but many of them drowned. A Latin inscription near the tomb of El Cid reads, "Brave and unconquered, famous in triumphs of war." Enclosed in this tomb lies Roderick the Great of Vivar. Babieca, loved by El Cid, also loved by the Christians and feared by his enemies, was buried in the monastery of San Pedro de Cardeña. According to Charles Petrie, in his *Introduction to Bertrand, History of Spain*:

> *The expulsion of the Moors has been the subject of romantic treatment at the hands of writers who exalt Mohammedan Spain and belittle the Christian tradition. The overthrow of Spanish Islam was written down as a definite calamity, and one from which unhappy Spain has never recovered. The anarchy which was continually breaking out even in the heyday of Omayyad power and the ferocity which marked the rule of the various Arab dynasties, were glossed over or altogether ignored, and a picture was painted which bore but a scanty resemblance to the truth.*

After his death on Sunday, July 10, 1099, El Cid's legend continued to grow. Roving minstrels sang ballads about his heroic deeds throughout the villages, and the most famous, titled "*El Cantar de Mío Cid*" (The Song of My Cid), was composed. These ballads were the forerunners of *corridos*, which praise or commemorate significant events and people. The minstrels sang the ballads to the tune of the lyre, which was a musical instrument that developed into what would be known as the Spanish guitar. It is interesting to note that in New Mexico people often refer to the guitar as *la lira*, the lyre.

The Moors were finally defeated when Don Fernando de Aragón and Doña Isabella de Castilla married. A united front gave birth to the country of Spain, with the capitulation of Granada and the meeting of the opposing armies in Santa Fé in 1492 finally ending a war that had lasted nearly eight hundred years.

The Black Plague

According to Melissa Snell in *The Spread of the Black Death through Europe*:

> *The first recorded appearance of the plague in Europe was at Messina, Sicily in October of 1347. Spain was in the midst of turmoil: there was armed rebellion in Aragón, and Christian Castile was engaged in a conflict*

with Moorish Granada. Christian merchants were attacked by Tartars at Kaffa…Before breaking off their attack they catapulted dead plague victims into the city in the hopes of infecting its residents…The defenders tried to divert the pestilence by throwing the bodies into the sea…but its doom was sealed…By June of 1348, nearly half of Europe had met the Black Death in one form or another…In Spain and Portugal, the plague crept inland from the port cities at a somewhat slower pace than in Italy and France. In the war at Granada, the Muslim soldiers were the first to succumb to the illness…the Christian enemies were also struck down by the hundreds…It was in Spain that the only ruling monarch to die of the disease met his end. The advisors of King Alfonse XI of Castile begged him to isolate himself, but he refused to leave his troops. He fell ill and died on March 26, 1350 on Good Friday.

The Progenitor: Doña Isabella de Castilla

Isabella was born in the heart of Iberia on April 22, 1451, as the direct descendant of the kings and queens of Castile, Portugal and England. In AD 981, Castilla became an independent country, and in 1004 it was raised

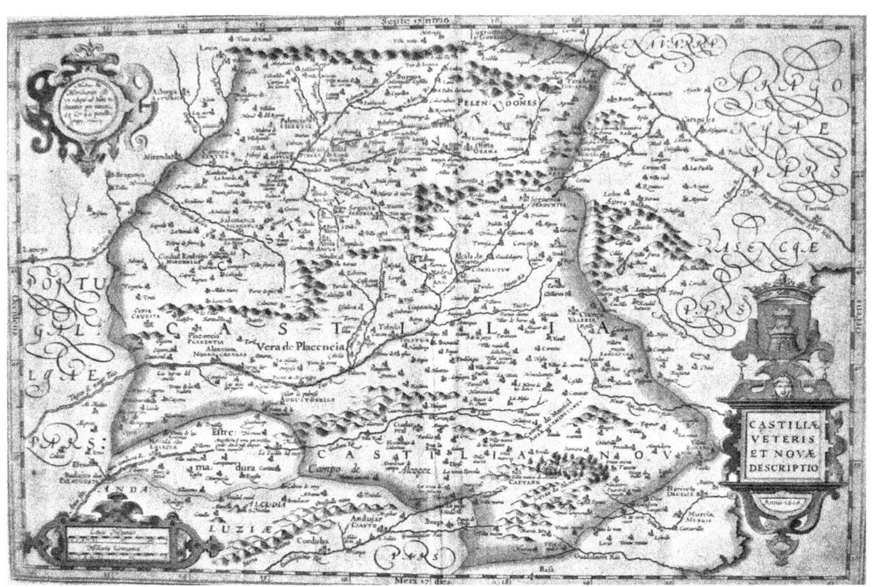

Castiliæ Veteris et Novæ Descriptio, Anno 1606, Meridianus. Map of Castilla, Spain. *Courtesy of the author.*

to the dignity of a kingdom. The nobles from León belittled the Castellanos by calling them pig farmers because they raised pigs and had *matanzas*.

Isabella of Castilla, like her ancestors, was tough, ready to face danger and hardship and willing to suffer hunger and to fight against great odds to defend her Christian faith and country. In the beginning, the people were one. Brilliant leaders rose among them, but everyone's status was equal. Eventually, things changed. By Isabella's time, many of the kings and queens of Castile had become weak, greedy and power hungry, as had happened in other parts of Europe. King John II and his second wife, Isabella of Portugal, Isabella of Castilla's parents, followed the political practices of the monarchy, and Isabella, like all children of royalty, became a pawn to be used to gain more land, political power and riches. The Royal Council, which consisted of powerful people of the nobility, made most of the country's major decisions, while the monarchy was satisfied mingling with one another in their luxurious lifestyles. Murder, bribery and corruption were commonplace in general society, and in many instances, church leaders mirrored the world around them.

Isabella was three years old, and her brother, Alfonso, was two years younger, when King John II died in 1454. King John II left money in his will for his wife and two children to live comfortably. He had a son, Henry IV, who inherited the crown after his death. Henry IV was King John's son from his first marriage to María de Aragón, the oldest daughter of King Ferdinand I of Aragón and his wife, Eleanor of Alburquerque. King Henry IV was already married to Joan of Portugal at the time of his father's death, but they had no children. King John II named Isabella heir to the throne if for any reason Henry IV could not fulfill his obligation. John also left majority custody of Isabella and Alfonso to Henry, since their mother, Isabella of Portugal, was considered to be mentally ill. Henry ignored the will of his father and sent Isabella and Alfonso to live with their mother in a castle that was in need of repair. Their mother was a staunch Catholic with ties to the Dominican Order, and even though she was ill, she wanted Isabella well versed in the Catholic religion and ingrained with the original ideals of the Castilian people.

Isabella and her brother were well educated, but they lived in poverty. They suffered, worked and struggled to survive. In the meantime, Joan of Portugal, Henry's wife, became pregnant. Henry sent for Isabella and Alfonso to come to his castle so he could keep a closer eye on them. The nobles forced him to sign an agreement making Isabella heir to the crown. They did not believe the child Joan was carrying was the king's. Henry's first marriage to Blanche of Aragón at the age of fifteen had never been consummated, and his marriage had been dissolved. Blanche was returned to her family, where she was imprisoned and later killed. Joan, Henry's present wife, was known to have had many illicit relationships. When Princess Joanna was born, Henry IV began plotting to marry off nine-year-old Isabella so that he could make Princess Joanna heir to the crown. King John II had promised Isabella in marriage to Fernando of Aragón before his death, but Henry wanted a match that would better serve his goals. Henry IV continued to make secret plans to marry Isabella to someone of his choice, but she turned down each suitor, and he could not force her to accept the proposals. Even threats of putting her in prison could not persuade her to accept the marriage arrangements.

King Henry IV became more disorganized with his rule over his kingdom. The kingdom was in severe debt, and he failed to enforce the laws. The nobles requested that Isabella take the crown by force. She refused, insisting that it was her brother Alfonso's birthright. King Henry eventually named Alfonso as heir to the crown. Just before Alfonso's crowning, the boy suddenly died. Instead of overthrowing King Henry IV in war, as the Royal Council advised, Isabella preferred to negotiate. Isabella gave up Portugal to Princess Joanna. The young queen made a secret promise to the king of Aragón to honor her father's original contract to marry his son Fernando of Aragón. She left the castle in secret to fulfill her promise of marriage at the age of fifteen.

The birth of Spain as a country in the fifteenth century took place when Queen Isabella of Castilla married King Fernando of Aragón on October 19, 1469, in Ocaña. With the personal union of the Castilian and Aragónese crowns, Castilla, Aragón, Catalonia and Valencia remained constitutionally distinct political entities, and they retained separate councils of state and parliaments. Each also had its own line of succession to the crown. Isabella de Castilla proved to be a fearless sword-wielding monarch in command of and at the head of her own army. She combined her forces with those of her husband, and together they were able to defeat the Moors at Granada. When the wars were over and the Reconquista was complete, the queen could concentrate on the people.

Isabella wanted to empower the people of Castilla to take pride in their country and put an end to the injustice and corruption brought about when subjects could settle disputes by the amount of money they were willing to use to make things go their way. The people of Castilla had once policed the roads and countryside for the kings of León and kept them safe; now,

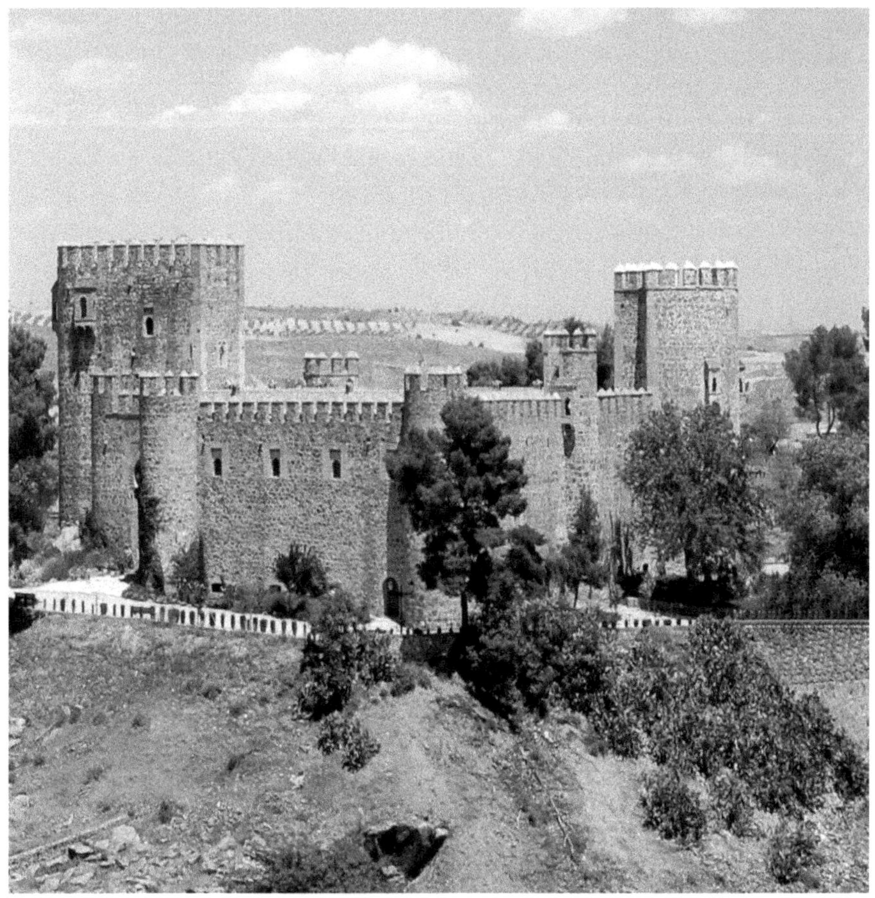

A medieval castle in Toledo, Spain. *Photograph ©Ramón Juan Carlos de Aragón, 2011.*

their tax money would pay an appointed police force and standing army—La Santa Hermandad (the Holy Brotherhood)—to ensure they were protected from tyrant nobles. The Hermandad consisted of local men of the middle class in positions of trust. Isabella felt this would put an end to the thief-infested nobility of the region. Land that King Henry IV had sold at under value would be restored to the people, and the money would be returned to the purchaser. Land that he had given away to pay for favors would be returned at no cost. The only gifts that did not need to be returned were those given to churches, hospitals or the poor. King Henry had given authority to different businesses to mint money to the point that the coin had very little value. Coinage would no longer be allowed, except under royal control, and a fixed legal standard was set. The queen also changed the power of the Royal

Council to the role of advisors, and they were no longer paid for their services. The judicial branch of the council was completely dissolved. The famous jurist Alfonso Díaz de Montalvo compiled the Ordenanzas Reales (the codes of law), and these were used to make all legal decisions. King Fernando of Aragón and Queen Isabella of Castilla were also available to the people every Friday for audiences similar to what we would today call town hall meetings. Queen Isabella felt it was important that her leadership as a monarch should be one where she would have a relationship with her subjects.

Spain began to prosper and soon became a world power. The king and queen had a love of country and church, but they also loved their children. Their motivation in each of their children's marriages was to make them allies in world affairs. Fernando and Isabella had grown up in a royal world where heirs to the throne were pitted against one another, and they didn't want that for their children. Their son and heir to the crown, Juan of Asturias, was born in 1478. Isabella set up a school at the castle so that her son could be educated. Juan loved singing and could play several instruments. He married the Archduchess Margaret of Austria in April 1497. Margaret was pregnant when Juan became seriously ill. Soon after, the future heir to the crown and only son of Fernando and Isabella died. Margaret gave birth to their stillborn girl.

Isabella, Princess of Asturias, born in 1470, became heir to the throne after the death of her brother in 1490. She married Alfonso, Crown Prince of Portugal, in 1490, and she was very happy. After a fall from his horse, Alfonso died, and Isabella became depressed and said she would never marry again. Her parents insisted that she marry Manuel I, King of Portugal, in 1497. A few hours after the birth of their son, Miguel de Paz, in 1498, Isabella died, and in 1500, Miguel de Paz also died at the age of two. Isabella's sister, María of Aragón, then married Manuel I. María and Manuel had ten children, including King John III and the Empress Isabella, wife of Emperor Charles V. Due to the death of her sister Isabella and brother Juan, and being the older sister of María, Joanna now became heir to the Spanish kingdoms.

Joanna, born in 1479, was the third child of Fernando and Isabella. History refers to her as "Joanna the Mad" or "Juana la Loca." Joanna outlived all of her siblings and died at the age of seventy-six in 1555. She was a tremendously gifted woman who mastered all of the Iberian Romance languages of Castilian, Leonese, Galician-Portuguese and Catalán, as well as being fluent in French and Latin. Joanna was also considered exceedingly attractive, with blue eyes and reddish blond hair. Fernando and Isabella arranged for her to be married to Philip the Handsome at the age of sixteen. Philip's parents were Holy Roman Emperor Maximilian I and his first wife, Duchess Mary of Burgundy. Joanna gave birth to six children: Emperor Charles V; Emperor Ferdinand I; Mary, Queen of Hungary; Isabella, Queen of Denmark; Catherine, Queen of Portugal; and Eleanor, Queen of Portugal and France. Philip was unfaithful from the beginning, and his mistreatment of her included having her imprisoned at a nunnery after claiming she was insane. Philip then placed himself as ruler of Castilla and Aragón and threatened to go to war against Fernando if he meddled in governmental affairs. Philip suddenly died, and Joanna refused to rule. Her father, King Fernando, served as regent of Castilla until her son Charles came of age.

Fernando and Isabella's last child was Catalina (Catherine) de Aragón, born in 1485. She is considered the most beloved queen in English history and was a leading intellectual, along with friends like Sir Thomas Moore and Erasmus. Thomas Moore wrote treatises in favor of higher education for women, which was strictly discouraged in England. King Henry VIII eventually ordered Moore's execution. Erasmus was also an influential writer of this period. Catherine's first marriage in 1501 was to Arthur, Prince of Wales, the oldest son of King Henry VII. After his death in 1502, she married his brother, Henry VIII, who then inherited the throne and was a first cousin of Queen Isabella of Castilla. They were happily married for several years and had six children, but only Mary I lived to adulthood.

Henry became infatuated with a younger woman, Anne Boleyn. The Catholic Church refused to sanction a divorce from Catherine, which Henry requested, so he established the Church of England. King Henry VIII married six times. King Henry ordered the execution of Anne Boleyn and his fifth wife, Kathryn Howard. He divorced Catherine of Aragón and his fourth wife, Anne of Cleves. His third wife died in childbirth, and then Henry finally died, leaving Katherine Parr a widow. Some say Henry VIII was about to have Katherine executed when he suddenly died.

Catherine's mother, Queen Isabella, was a woman of great determination, resourcefulness, ability and courage. She proved by example that a woman could rule successfully in a male-dominated world. Catherine followed her lead with dignity, never giving up her title as queen of England, and was the only person to stand up to Henry VIII and not lose her life. She passed on this courage to her daughter, Mary I, Queen of Scotland, who eventually became a leader in her own right. Isabella, in spite of her sorrow over witnessing the loss or struggles of her children, led Spain through the

Spanish golden age of exploration and colonization with the voyages of Columbus and sat at the helm of the first modern world power.

Through a stroke of luck, Queen Isabella found out about Columbus through her confessor, Padre Hernando Talavera, just before the explorer was to leave Spain, and she asked to see him. Columbus explained his idea about crossing the Atlantic Ocean to reach the Orient on the other side of the world to get spices that were worth their weight in gold. Spices were important to the people. The reason for this was that food wasn't refrigerated in those days. Food would get a bad taste after a short time, so spices covered up the bad taste. Spices not only made food taste better but also helped to preserve it. It was difficult to get the spices by land since the journey to the Orient was through desert terrain or areas controlled by marauding bandits. Queen Isabella, a visionary, saw the value of Columbus's plan. The remarkable queen financed what would be perhaps the greatest journey of exploration in the history of the world.

Queen Isabella la Catolica, the "Catholic Queen," changed the direction of the Old World and led it into the New World. The marvelous queen directed the discovery, conquest and settlement of the Americas and other parts of the world. She led the largest evangelization movement of the Catholic Church in history, after the apostles. She was instrumental in defeating the Moorish occupation of Spain after eight hundred years of dominance. Queen Isabella promoted the emancipation of women and the equality of women in all leadership roles, including the family, the church, the state and government. Historically, she believed in universal human rights, and she was way ahead of her time and place. The historian and writer Andrés Bernáldez (1450–1513) wrote about Queen Isabella of Castilla: "She was an endeavored woman, very powerful, very prudent, wise, very honest, chaste, devout, discreet, truthful, clear, without deceit. Who could count the excellences of this very Catholic and happy Queen, always very worthy of praises."

Conquistadoras

Following the example of Queen Isabella, most Spanish women who arrived in the harsh foreign land of New Mexico during the colonial period were strong-willed and determined. These women of Spanish origin who carried forth their love of Spanish history, heritage, traditions and culture preserved and promoted much of the Spanish culture that survives today in New

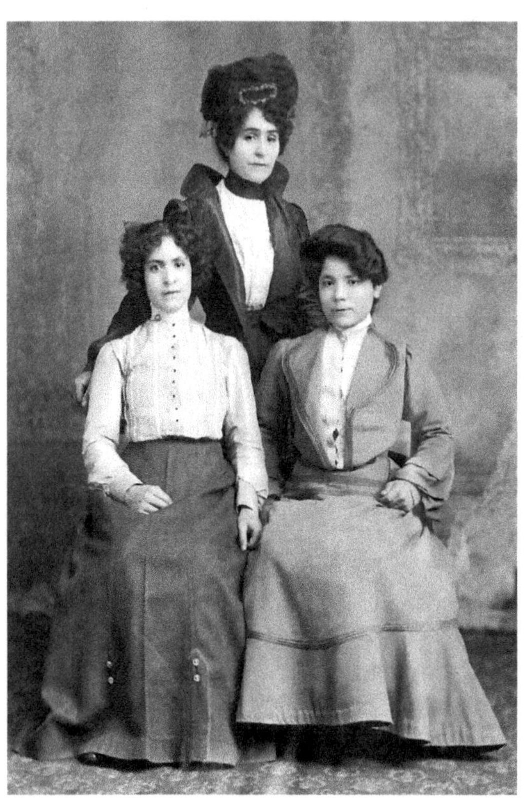

Left: Doña Rosalía Castellano Mondragón with daughters Luz and Margarita. *James Furlong photo, circa 1878. Courtesy of the author.*

Below: A Las Vegas, New Mexico family. James Furlong photo, circa 1880. *Courtesy of the author.*

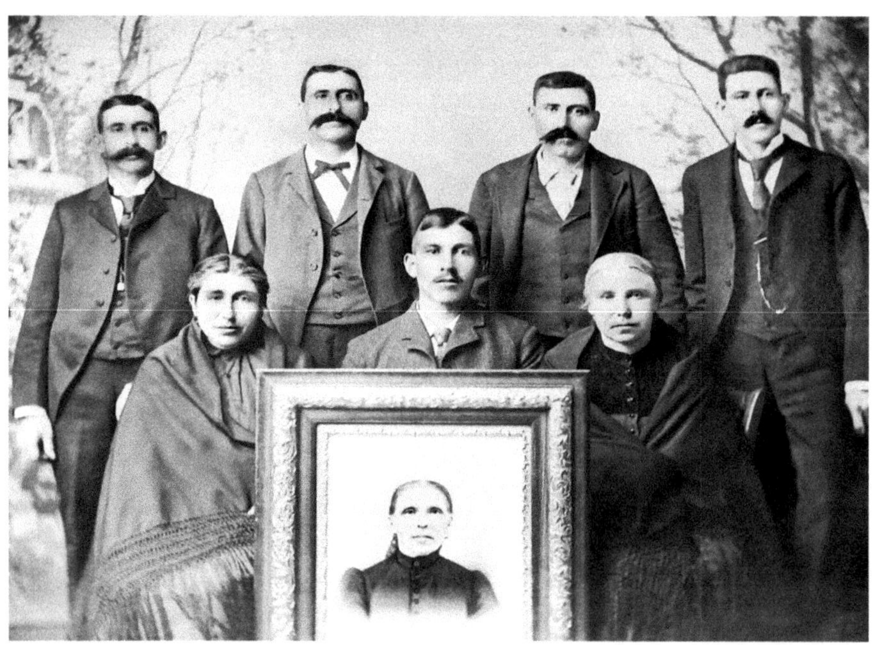

Mexico. The reality is that Spanish women not only served as the backbone of their families and the movers and shakers in society, but they also stood at the forefront in defense of their children and were courageous in battle.

During Spanish exploration and settlement of the Americas, Spanish women left their imprint on the soil. María Velasquez de Cuellar and ten other women accompanied the Pánfilo de Narvaez Expedition that sailed into Boca Ciega Bay in 1528. Francesca de Henestrosa traveled with the famous de Soto Expedition in 1539 that discovered the Mississippi. In 1582, Doña Casilda de Anaya journeyed with the Don Antonio de Espejo Expedition into New Mexico, along with her husband, Don Miguel Sánchez Valenciano, and their three children.

La Conquistadora, Doña Catalina de Erauso, born in the village of San Sebastian, the daughter of Captain Don Miguel de Erauso and Doña María Perez de Galarraga y Arce, in 1585, had unmatched skills with a sword. She fought for the Spanish Empire in Peru and Chile against the Indians in the early seventeenth century. She took on the alias of Francisco Loyola and became a legend in her own time. She wrote an autobiography about her adventures. Her book was so popular that it went into two printings. She returned to Spain, and a popular play was written about her.

In 1610, Don Gaspar Pérez de Villagrá published his marvelous epic poem, *Historia de la Nueva México* (History of the New Mexico). Villagrá, in one of his *cantos* (heroic stanzas), wrote about Doña Eufemia de Sosa, the wife of Alférez (standard-bearer) Don Francisco Sosa de Peñalosa. His long poem about the establishment of a Spanish colony in New Mexico in 1598 mentioned a near battle with the Indians at San Juan de los Caballeros, the first Spanish capital. The men prepared to defend the fledgling colony. Doña Eufemia, along with her daughter and twenty-two other women, armed and fortified the rooftops of their homes. This very courageous woman inspired the colonists in a famous speech to persevere in settling the territory, and she championed the building of a great city when some of the men thought of abandoning the colony. No monument stands today honoring the bravery of this woman in Spanish New Mexican history.

After the independence of Mexico in 1821, the Mexican government passed a civil code that systematically abolished and severely restricted women's rights. This had little or no effect in New Mexico, where the inhabitants considered themselves to be virtually independent of the Republic.

Exploration, El Camino Real and the Franciscans

Those who embrace the uniqueness of the land and its indigenous cultures call New Mexico the "Land of Enchantment." Spanish explorers were traveling from one end to another of the newly acquired lands of the Americas long before Spanish settlement. New Mexico's mountainous wonders and beautiful valleys captivated explorers and travelers who saw their awesome splendor. The soul of the land was felt through the sacred dances and rituals of the Indians, and their music filled the skies with vibrant voices and melodious songs. The deep devotion to "Mother Earth" and "Father Sky" flowed from the hearts of the Indians as they danced and sang their praises for life and being. They lived with the land, and the land lived with them. And so it was for the Spanish settlers who traveled along an early Indian trail they called *El Camino Real*, the "Royal Road."

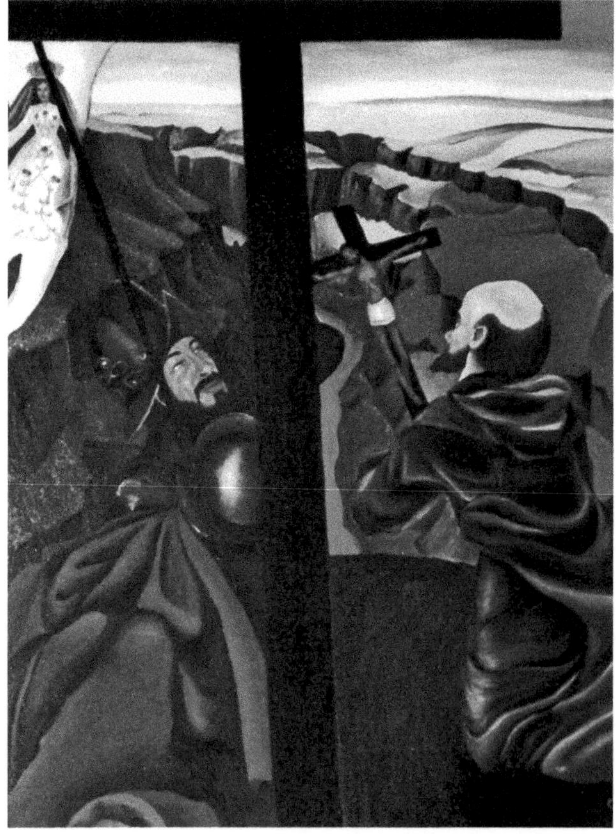

La Santa Fé. Oil on canvas. ©*Rosa María Calles.*

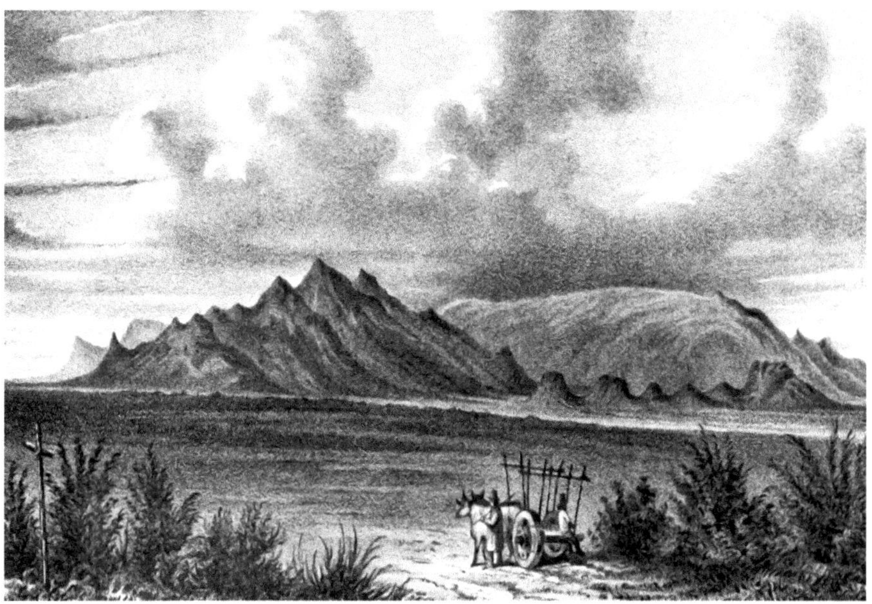

El Camino Real Near Santa Fé, Showing Descanso. Engraving, unknown engraver. *Courtesy of the author.*

El Camino Real was one of the most significant early trade routes connecting Native Americans of the great Southwest. For hundreds, perhaps thousands, of years, the Indians traded turquoise, shells, beads, exotic feathers and foodstuffs while traveling to and from northern Mexico to present-day New Mexico. Recent discoveries are adding to the wealth of research that we currently have about this trail. Early Native Americans may have used this route to exchange ideas that focused on religion, philosophy, architectural building techniques, the arts and even styles of dress and customs. The impact of this major trade route rose and fell with early Southwest Indian civilizations, as they dealt with war, famine and drought. The route continued unabated for centuries as a very powerful lifeline, ranking in importance with other roads and trails that had an impact on the history and course of mankind.

When Spanish explorers arrived on the North American continent in the sixteenth century and traveled on their journeys of discovery, they found it was much easier to follow trails that Native Americans had used for generations before them. With guides leading the way, the Spanish knew where the areas of danger were located, where watering holes and wild game were to be found and where the native villages were centered. Spanish cartographers mapped the way so that the colonization process could begin. Once it was firmly established on maps as an officially recognized and decreed road, the Spanish government utilized El Camino Real for military campaigns and excursions, for the transportation of goods and livestock and for the establishment of settlements.

One early Spanish explorer was Ponce de León, who searched for the Fountain of Youth and discovered Florida in 1513. He was one of the first Europeans to set foot on North American soil while seeking out an Indian mythological site that was said to contain miraculous water that could restore youth and vitality. In 1528, Alvar Nuñez Cabeza de Vaca, an explorer and survivor of the ill-fated Narvaez Expedition, which was shipwrecked off the coast of Galveston, Texas, was joined by other surviving adventurers, including Estebanico, an Arabic Moor.

Cabeza de Vaca may have been the first European to arrive in New Mexico around 1535. An interesting story is told about his surname. During the Middle Ages, when the Arabic Moors were fighting the Spanish, a sheepherder marked the spot where the Moorish enemy had crossed the river with a cow's skull. A Spanish king and his valiant knights crossed the river where the skull served as a marker, catching the Moors by surprise and defeating them in a major battle. The king knighted the sheepherder, giving him the surname Cabeza de Vaca for his family to carry on as a great honor.

A talent that Alvar Nuñez Cabeza de Vaca had was for being a healer. He may have inherited this knowledge from a sheepherding family, since every shepherd had to know how to heal himself while out tending flocks. After swimming ashore, de Vaca and his companions were captured by the Indians following the shipwreck. The Indians sold him and the others from one tribe to another as slaves. Stories of de Vaca's powers to heal circulated among the tribes. It was said that an Indian chief's daughter became gravely ill. The chief promised freedom for de Vaca and his friends if he could save her. Cabeza de Vaca checked the girl and determined a cure, and she was miraculously saved. The chief released the Spaniards, and de Vaca established a reputation among the Indians as a great medicine man with miraculous powers.

The wanderers finally made their way to the city of Mexico, where Alvar Nuñez Cabeza de Vaca told stories about wonderful cities they had seen or heard of, and he wrote a book about his great adventures. Stories he heard from the natives included tales of cities with houses that gleamed with gold, sapphires and turquoise. Due to the stories and the excitement aroused by the book, Viceroy Antonio de Mendoza sent out an expedition to search for cities of gold to be found somewhere in New Mexico. Fray Marcos de Niza, a Franciscan friar who had experience exploring South and Central America, led the expedition. The fray took Estebanico as a guide and then sent him on ahead of the group to scout and report back. Estebanico was instructed by the fray to send him a cross as a sign of any discoveries. The size of the cross would determine the importance of his findings. After four days, Estebanico sent back messengers who carried a cross "as high as man." The Spanish priest was certain this meant fabulous riches.

Fray Marcos de Niza was elated and pushed forward to get to the pueblo of Hawikuh. He arrived there in May 1539. Fray Marcos discovered that the Indians had killed Estebanico, but this did not keep him from claiming the land, raising a flag and erecting a cross in the name of Spain. Fray Marcos returned to Mexico City and told of wealthy cities in the north that were full of gold. He based his stories on Estebanico's large cross, which to him was a clear indication of incomparable riches to be found in New Mexico. Another expedition was sent. A very bold and courageous leader, Don Francisco Vásquez de Coronado, commanded the expedition. This enormous expedition included many soldiers, some Spanish women who accompanied their husbands, Indian servants, provisions, numerous horses and cattle. Among the women were María Maldonado, María Caballero and Francisca de Hozes.

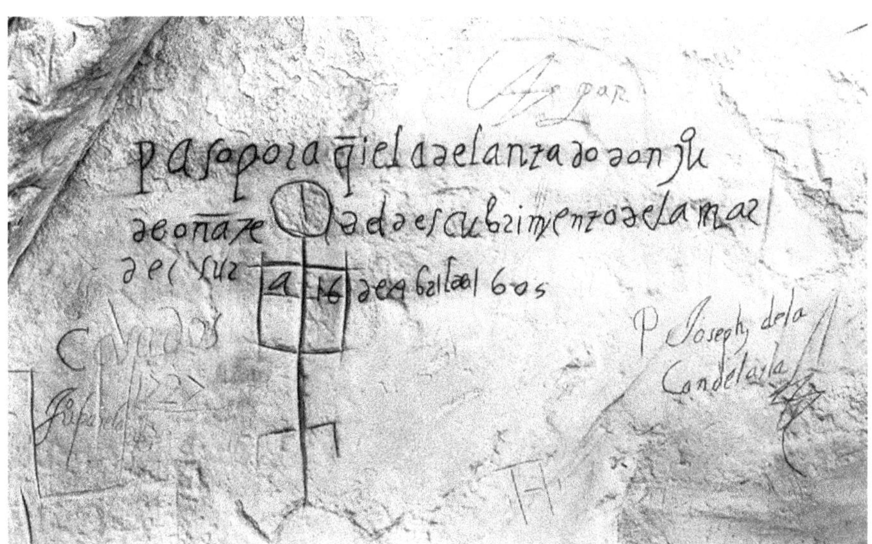

Oñate inscription at El Morro National Monument. Photographer and date unknown. *Courtesy of the author.*

Although no riches were found, Don Juan de Oñate y Salazar followed Coronado by leading a large group of settlers to New Mexico in 1598. Oñate assembled a diverse group of men, women and children. They ranged from infants to a sixty-year-old. Women and children signed up to accompany their husbands or fathers. Several single women joined the pioneers. Since women and children were rarely counted, records are sparse as to how many there actually were. Logically, there had to have been several hundred to comply with the royal decree for establishment of a genuine settlement. Adult male recruits who could put down roots for five years would be awarded the title of Hidalgo. This was the lowest rank of nobleman. Oñate led an impressively large force. They also took with them eighty-three ox carts, twenty-four wagons, two of Oñate's personal carriages and approximately seven thousand head of livestock. Perez de Villagrá, who recorded the journey, defined the distribution of stock as including "oxen, a beef herd, swine, goats, donkeys, sheep, goats, horses, and mules." He wrote that the moving camp spread out for three miles in length along the trail and was just as wide. Reports indicate that there were about 400 men—129 of them soldiers, 150 with families and servants and 10 Franciscans.

The Franciscan frays who accompanied the settlers were extremely devoted to their church and faith, and they followed the mandate given by Queen Isabella to evangelize the Americas. Although the impact of their work and efforts was vast, very little has been written about them. Juan R. Véles Hidalgo, in *The Church in Spanish America and the Catholic Historical Review*, stated:

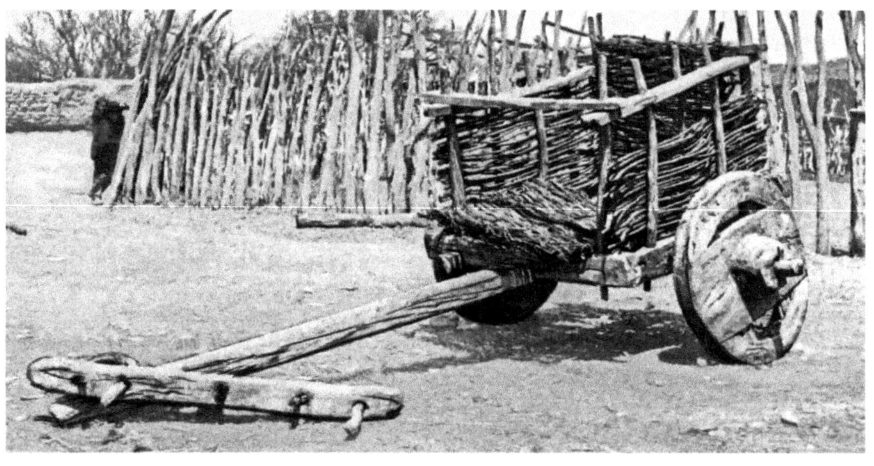

Carreta (ox cart), Detroit Publishing Co., circa 1900. Photographer unknown. *Courtesy of the author.*

> *The Church in America was almost ignored…The present day absence of journal articles on the Church History of the United States between the late 16th and mid 18th century, particularly the contribution of the Spanish orders and the Patronato Real is strikingly evident…Popular knowledge echoes today what one wrote in the first quarter of this century: "It is not often that a school history of the U.S. fails to describe the inhumanity of the Spaniards"…Although the same author later praises the achievements of some men such as Las Casas he fails to give credit to many other Spanish missionaries, bishops, and at times governors, who denounced the abuse of the natives, sought their protection, and introduced important spiritual and cultural contributions to the Indian cultures…Oddly there are no articles on Fr. Junipero Serra…most outstanding missionaries such as Fr. Germin Lasuen…Franciscan priests who opened and directed the missions of New Mexico at the start of the 17th century and the ones of Texas at the close of the same century…articles on the Church History in Spanish America vary greatly, including the capellanias, the black legend, the Bull Inter caetera, and nuns in colonial Mexico…Christopher Columbus and the motives for voyaging to America, his writing on prophecies and the funding for his voyages. In light of the large number of institutions and figures in the history of the New World, this interest in Columbus seems disproportionately high…articles devoted to Bishop John Carroll, some to Catholic European immigrants, and a few to the French Jesuits. In these there is scant if any reference to the work of earlier Spanish missionaries. There is a marked absence of articles on the religious and social conditions of Indian tribes and especially the Indians partially evangelized by the Spanish…*[publications] *indicates that the early history of the Church in the U.S. is almost entirely limited to the history of the European immigrants who settled in the Eastern coast of North America. In addition, it suggests that the Spanish American missions in Florida, New Mexico, Texas and California are poorly known and have gained little attention among Church historians. A similar conclusion could be reached with regard to the religious fate of the Indians of these regions during the 19th century…reasons for this omission: historians have been biased against Spanish heritage in America.*

It cannot be disputed that the Franciscan movement in the Americas was responsible for the massive building of churches and for the evangelization and education of the Indians. Pope Julian II issued a bull in 1508 granting the Spanish crown a *pratronato real*; that is, the responsibility and duty of

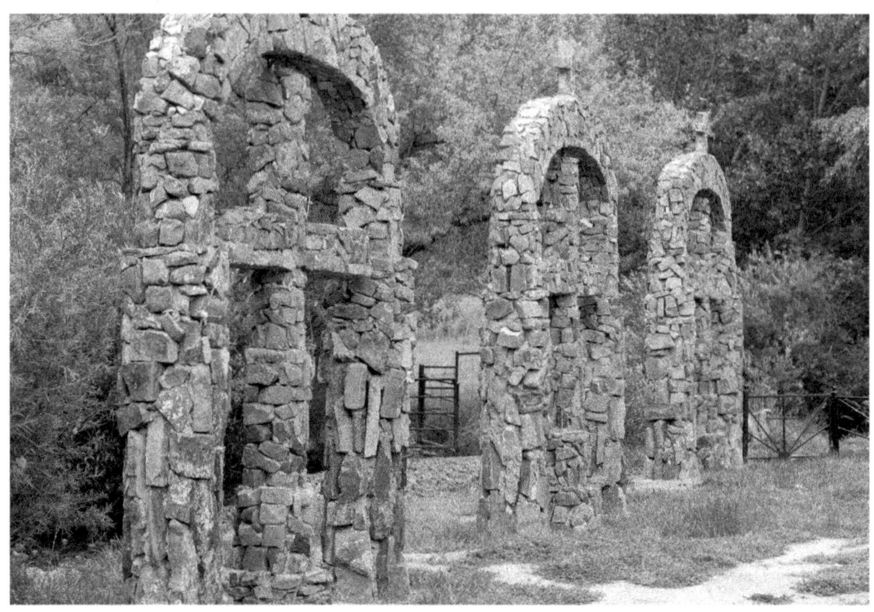

Chimayo. *Photograph ©Ramón Juan Carlos de Aragón, 2011.*

financially maintaining the spread of Christianity. Due to the papal bull, the humanitarian and faith-filled zeal of the frays who followed the example and teachings of Saint Francis of Assisi was unprecedented in human history. In many cases, the Franciscans set up guilds and schools along with the churches. In the guilds, the natives were taught the arts of painting, sculpting, gesso-relief, gilding and how to manufacture musical instruments. The associations of artisans working to help embellish the churches were often times joined by Spanish lay craftsmen and artists. Other skills, such as wool weaving and crafts to produce eating and farming utensils and silver and ironwork, were later added by the industrious frays. The schools run by the frays were the first bilingual schools in the Americas since the Indians knew their native tongues and learned Spanish as well.

The frays who arrived in New Mexico included Fray Francisco de Padilla, Fray Daniél, Fray Juan de la Crúz and Fray Luís de Escalona, all of whom traveled with Coronado's Expedition, remained in New Mexico and were martyred. One of Coronado's men wrote about Fray de la Cruz, "He was so highly regarded for his saintly life by Coronado himself, that the latter gave orders to his soldiers that each should touch his hat or helmet whenever the name of this Holy man was mentioned."

Fray Agustín Rodríguez led an expedition to explore the pueblo areas of New Mexico to establish missions. He was martyred. Fray Francisco López and Fray Juan de Santa María, who were with the group, were also martyred. Fray Francisco de Velasco and Fray Pedro de Vergara were with the Oñate settlers of 1598. Fray Juan de Salas was a missionary among the Tompiro and Jumano Indians of the Salinas region of New Mexico and built the Isleta Mission Church. He gained the admiration and respect of the Indians. Fray Diego López from León, Spain, was with him.

In 1626, Fray Alonzo de Benavides, Franciscan custos, arrived in New Mexico and produced his *Memoriales*, which were reports to the king on the ecclesiastical conditions of the viceroyalty of New Spain. Some of the frays claimed to Fray Benavides that a Spanish Conceptionist Franciscan nun, María de Jesús de Ágreda, the reverend mother and abbess of the Convento de la Purísima Concepción de Ágreda, was being miraculously translocated from Spain to the Provincias de Nuevo México to preach to the Indians in or about the year 1620. Many sick Indians were healed through her intercessions. Fray Benavides interviewed the reverend mother at her *convento* on his return to Spain and was stunned with her precise descriptions of New Mexico and the Indians to whom she ministered. In 1634, his *Memorial* was published in Madrid. Fray Ascención de Zárate and Fray Juan de Ortega ministered among the Jumanos in 1632. New Mexico's Socorro mission was founded by Fray García San Francisco y Zuñiga, and Fray Francisco de Ayates distinguished himself by providing desperately needed assistance at El Paso del Norte to the Spanish settlers fleeing New Mexico after the Revolt of 1680. Through his selfless efforts, he supplied them with food, clothing and other necessities that helped the colonists to settle.

With the resettlement of New Mexico by de Vargas in 1692, the Franciscan frays returned with the spiritual fervor of the apostles in the early church to spread throughout the New World the faith of their ancestors and root the church firmly for those who would come later to this transplanted Castillian land of Isabella. The Franciscan frays rebuilt the missions on the hallowed grounds filled with the precious spilt blood of their predecessors. During the following one hundred years, the imprint of the priests was woven through every single thread of the fabric of what we today call traditional Hispano New Mexico culture.

Native Americans

The Americas that Columbus found were populated with people the Spanish called "Indians" because they thought they had reached India. The Spanish called the new lands the West Indies. Spanish explorers came into contact with innumerable different and distinct Native American tribes as they traveled through South America, Central America and North America. They grouped the natives together under one name, but the truth of the matter is that the population was composed of hundreds of different and distinct groups with their own languages and diverse cultures. Some of these groups fought against one another constantly. The most powerful groups when Columbus sailed were the Aztecs of Tenochtitlan and the Incas of Peru.

Aztecs

The Aztecs settled on small islands in Lake Texcoco in 1325. According to legend, sun god Huitzilopochtli became divine king of the Aztecs in 1325 and ruled from the capital Tenochtitlan and its sister city Tlatelolco (today's Mexico City). As time passed, the Aztecs built up a truly remarkable civilization that extended through most of present-day Mexico. The Aztecs were successful in defeating dozens of other tribes, and they ruled the land with a firm and steady grip, demanding heavy taxes.

According to one of Hernán Cortés's men, Bernal Diaz del Castillo, who recorded the events of the expedition, Cortés arrived with 508 soldiers on eleven ships, 100 sailors, sixteen horses and a few cannons, crossbows and other pieces of artillery. They named the landing site Veracruz, the "True Cross." The Spaniards were awakened each morning by the screams of sacrificial victims. Cortés told Montezuma to stop, but he would not. The Spaniards were appalled at the horrible spectacle of human sacrifice. Aztecs were consumed and overcome with fear of the supernatural and superstition. Needless to say, the captive tribes did not like the idea that thousands of their young braves and maidens—and sometimes even children—needed to be sacrificed to the war god Huitzilopochtli and the sun god Quetzalcoatl to keep the Aztec gods happy. The Aztecs really did believe that if people weren't sacrificed on the day before, then the sun would not come up on the next day and the world would plunge into eternal darkness. Of course, at one time, Europeans thought the world was flat and that if you traveled too far out on the ocean you would fall down into nothingness.

In 1519, war broke out, and Cortés, with 500 Spanish soldiers and 170,000 Indians who had been dominated and oppressed by the Aztecs, defeated the Aztec Empire, which had 180,000 warriors. The oppressed Indians had wanted to revolt for some time, but they did not have the right leadership. Cortés provided them with that opportunity and leadership. Francisco Pizarro, with the help of dominated and oppressed Indians, defeated the Inca Empire in Peru a few years later.

OUR LADY OF GUADALUPE

The Franciscan frays were having a hard time converting the Indians in the valley of Mexico after the conquest, and many of them were being martyred. The Aztecs and other tribes were constantly rebelling against the Spanish. Then a miracle took place in 1530 in which Mary, the mother of Jesus, appeared to a native of Mexico whose Christian name was Juan Diego.

In December 1530, Mary (Our Lady of Guadalupe) asked Juan Diego to collect *Rosas de Castilla* (Castilian roses) from a rocky hill as proof of her appearances. The roses were indigenous to Castile, Spain, and were not known in the New World. Diego went to the bishop and told him that the mother of Jesus wanted a church to be built on the spot where she had appeared to him. The bishop did not believe him. According to tradition, San Juan Diego opened up his *tilma* (cloak), which he used to collect the flowers, and a miraculous image of Mary was imprinted in their place. The appearance of the roses in the middle of winter was a miracle in itself. This

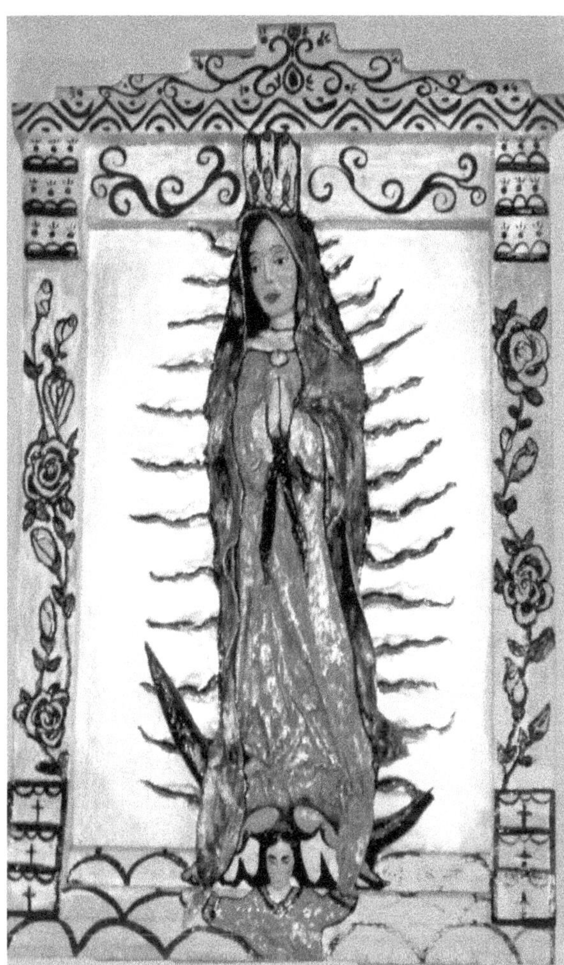

Our Lady of Guadalupe.
Mixed media, Ray John de Aragón.

event is recorded in history in the *Nican Mopohua*, written in Náhuatl about 1540 by Bishop Colégio de la Santa Cruz. The Codex 1548, drawings of the apparition of Our Lady of Guadalupe, was discovered in 1995 in a private collection. The Codex signed by Don Antonio Valeriano and his teacher, Father Bernardino de Sahagún, has a date of 1548, and it was scientifically determined to be genuine. It substantiates the historical basis of the apparition of Our Lady of Guadalupe. Many miracles were attributed to the apparition, but most significant was the conversion of over eight million Aztec Indians to Catholicism in the following seven years.

Spanish-controlled areas of the Western Hemisphere were divided up into two viceroyalties headquartered in Mexico City and Lima, Peru. The title of viceroy was given to personal representatives of the king who wielded considerable power over the newly acquired territories. New Mexico fell under the jurisdiction of the viceroyalty of New Spain. Within a few short years after the discovery, hundreds of Castilians crossed the Atlantic to spread newly defined Spanish pride to the new hemisphere. Unfortunately, some of the Spanish arrived in Hispaniola deathly ill. Present-day Cuba was called Hispaniola. In 1516, there was an outbreak of smallpox in Hispaniola, and from 1520 until 1524, the massive pandemic of this disease took the lives of more than 75 percent of the population. European diseases spread rapidly, and many Indians died. The Indians did not have the immune systems to fight off the diseases brought from the Old World.

Explorations of the newly acquired territories spread rapidly. Many Indian civilizations had risen and fallen like those of the Egyptians, Greeks and Romans in Western history. The Olmec and the Mayans, for example, built temple pyramids that compare to those erected by the Egyptians. The Mayans developed hieroglyphics, the mathematical concept of zero and astronomical observatories like those built by the astounding Olmec. People who had developed extraordinary cultures inhabited the New World. These "Indians" had achieved tremendous technological advances during different periods of history.

Some tribes were very primitive and lived as Stone Age hunters and gathers, in contrast to others who lived under luxurious conditions in sumptuous surroundings. It was the wealthier and more powerful tribes that subjugated and controlled those who were weaker, and they pressed them into slavery and servitude. At the time of the arrival of Columbus, Native Americans were segregated by both poverty and wealth. Queen Isabella of Castilla wanted the natives to be treated with honor, respect and dignity. She also pushed for the enforcement of strict penalties against anyone caught abusing the Indians' rights. It was through her that the Council of the Indies was established in 1503 as a governmental unit organized as the Secretariat of Indian Affairs, with broad powers to protect the Native Americans. The queen had so much concern and sympathy for the Indians that she alone established laws for their protection, giving them all the rights afforded to Spanish citizens. She also mandated that the Indians should be educated.

The first university on the American continent was founded in Mexico City in 1551. Mexico was also the site of the first school that specifically served to teach the Indians languages and the arts. The frays also learned to speak the languages of the Native American people. They did not force their Castilian language on the Indians. The Indians learned European artistic elements, which they combined with their own techniques while producing paintings, ceramics, textiles and lacquer work. This helped to develop a unique Mexican Baroque style. The first printing house and the first mint to produce coins were also established in Mexico City. This was accomplished in spite of the bubonic plague, which ravished Mexico from 1545 until 1548. American Indian Felipe Guaman Poma de Ayala (Quechua) illustrated his 1,189-page book, *La Primer Nueva Crónica y Buen Gobierno*, from 1600 until 1615. The plague was spreading in Europe and reached Madrid by 1599; it arrived in the southern city of Seville by 1600. Valencia lost an estimated 30,000 people. By the time it was over in Spain, almost 700,000 lives had been lost.

Encomienda

In the provinces of New Spain, some areas were named after the provinces of Spain, such as Nuevo León and La Nueva Galicia. Another practice adopted from Spain was the system of *encomiendas* (grants of land placed in trust), which was in effect in Spain since the Reconquista of 1492. After the reconquest of Spain, *adelantados*, governors of a province, could extract tribute from the Moors. The Spanish crown instituted the system of encomienda to regulate Indian labor in the Americas. In essence, those in charge of encomiendas had to instruct natives in the Spanish language and the Roman Catholic faith and protect them from any warring tribes. However, *encomenderos* (governors) in the New World could not own Indian land, in contrast to the encomenderos in Spain, who could. The Spanish crown of Castile had exclusive rights of administration, so harsh penalties were extracted on those who abused those rights—though in some cases natives were forced to do hard labor in mines and fields, akin to slavery of blacks in New England. However, if caught, adelantados in Spanish colonies would be forced to walk naked in the streets of Mexico City and Peru, and they would be stripped of all titles and possessions if they abused the natives in any way. Their disgrace would then pass on from that dark day to their descendants.

The quasi-feudal system of encomiendas persisted in Mexico until the revolution of 1821, but the practice had been abolished all the way back to 1720 in most Spanish-controlled areas, even in the territory of Santa Fé. It had come to pass that grantees of encomiendas could be conquistadores and soldiers, but notable Indians, Spanish women and Indian women could

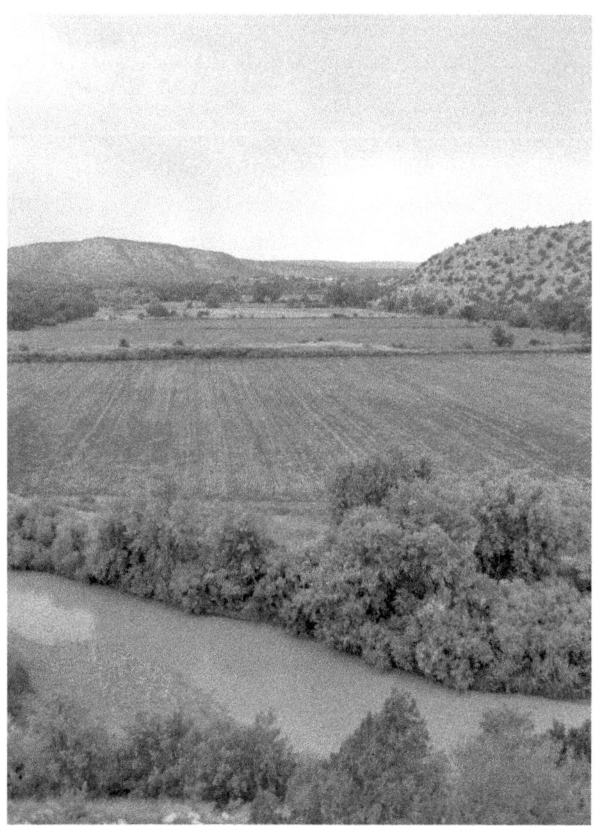

Left: Acequia. *Photograph ©Ramón Juan Carlos de Aragón, 2011.*

Below: Segovia. *Photograph ©Ramón Juan Carlos de Aragón, 2011.*

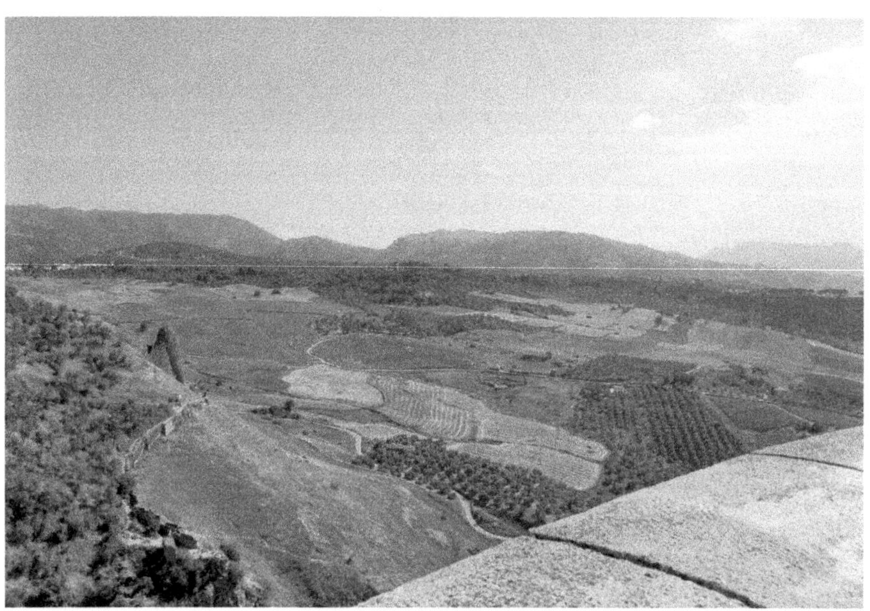

be recipients of titles as well. La Malinche and the daughters of the Aztec Montezuma received extensive encomiendas as dowries. Incan rulers also eyed encomiendas. Indentured Indian labor was supposed to end when the Spanish crown tried to put an end to the encomienda system. The Repartamiento and hacienda systems, which were large landed estates, were put in place of the encomienda.

In New Mexico, there were several haciendas: those of Don Pedro Durán de Chávez and his sons, Nicolas and Fernando, and the Don Severino Martínez hacienda. Don Severino's hacienda in Taos, New Mexico, is a living ranch today. With the Repartamiento, land ownership was more profitable, and displaced Indians called Genizaros—those who had lost families through Indian raids—were raised on haciendas until emancipation, when they could marry or join Indians of their own tribes.

The Pueblos and Missions

The Pendejo Cave people had been in New Mexico since about 10,000 BC. The inhabitants of the Sandia Cave and Clovis were ancient civilizations of New Mexico. The Clovis people were skilled hunters with knowledge of plants for food and had finely crafted tools. The Anasazi migrated into New Mexico sometime after AD 450 and left their homes in AD 1100. The Anasazi constructed elaborately carved dwellings and stone structures high atop cliff walls. They also had distinctive styles of pottery and baskets. Then the Pueblo people migrated into the Río Grande Valley about AD 1300. Approximately forty thousand people lived in sixty villages, where they built two- and three-story buildings that could have as many as three hundred rooms. The first floor did not have entrances or exits; instead, residents climbed up and in on ladders. This was to protect them against Apache attacks.

The Golden Age for the New Mexico missions and the building of churches began in 1610, and by 1816 one hundred churches had been built. Only one of these churches was expected to serve the colonists. The Santa Clara Indians, descendants of the inhabitants of the ancient Puyé Cliff dwellers near Española, settled in the area in 1550. Other missions the Franciscan frays established included those in the Hopi Indian tribe areas of Arizona and New Mexico; Santo Domingo Pueblo near the Cerrillos turquoise mines (destroyed by the floods and later relocated); the San Miguel in Socorro; San Agustín de la Isleta; San Isidro at Grán Quivíra,

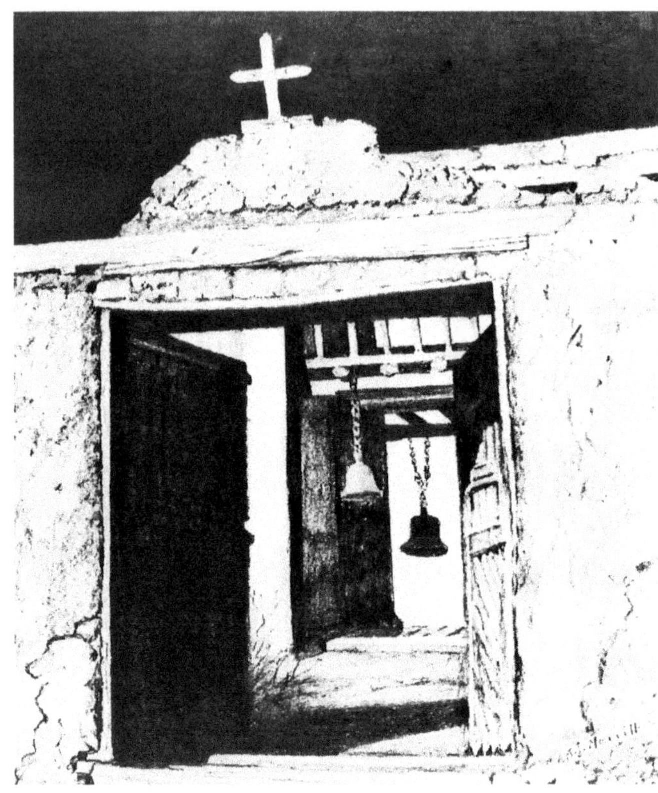

Las Trampas Church, Arthur J. Merrill, Taos, New Mexico. Photo postcard, unknown date. *Courtesy of the author.*

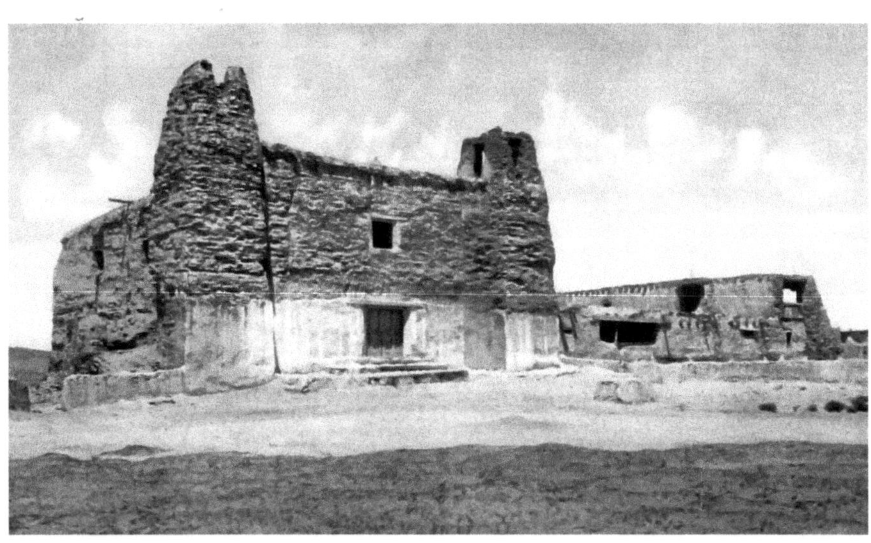

Acoma Pueblo Church, Detroit Publishing Co., circa 1902. Photo postcard. *Courtesy of the author.*

near Mountainair; San Buenaventura de Cochití; San Estevan del Rey de Acoma; San José (Giusewa) de Jémez; San José de La Laguna; Our Lady of Guadalupe in Zuni Pueblo; San Gregorio de Abó; Nuestra Señora de la Asunción de Zia; San Felipe; San Ildefonso; Santa Ana; Santuario de Guadalupe Church in Santa Fé; San Lorenzo de Picurís; the Santuario de Chimayo Church and many others. In 1709, Santa Ana Pueblo negotiated for and obtained five thousand acres and then fifteen thousand acres of Spanish land grants to establish their pueblo. The Jicarilla Apaches settled in the San Juan Mountains. Mescalero Apaches settled in the Ruidoso area. Fray Junipero Serra, one of the most famous of the order of Franciscans ministering among the Indians, set his sights on the expansion of the church in 1769. Serra established a string of twenty-one mission churches serving over thirty thousand Indians from Arizona to California. The church of San Javier del Bac in Tucson was established in 1776.

Indians under the Spanish government were able to maintain their uniqueness, although in some instances they incorporated some Spanish influences into their own and vice versa. This was primarily due to trade between the Indians and the Spanish. For example, in New Mexico, it was not altogether unusual to see Pueblo Indian arts and crafts—like clay pots, Navajo weaving and other handmade items—among the furnishings

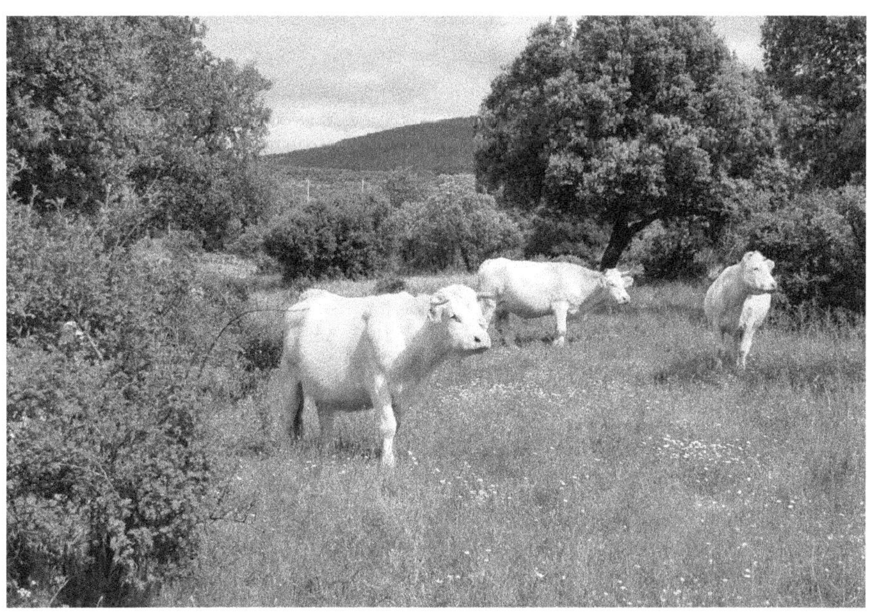

A Segovia pasture. *Photograph ©Ramón Juan Carlos de Aragón, 2011.*

of Spanish homes. The Indians likewise highly valued the painted wood panels, carved religious images and *hornos* that the Spanish colonists produced. Spanish colonists sometimes wore Indian moccasins called *teguas* and buckskin clothing. Indian women loved *rebozos*, the long-fringed shawls that Spanish women wore. They also liked the velvet blouses and cotton skirts. Indian women learned the art of spinning wool, weaving woolen blankets and making stockings. The interchange was continuous, and the development of Spanish culture in the New World was further enhanced by the Native American cultures. The Indians also felt positive influences from the Spanish way of life.

The Spanish introduced horses, burros, cattle, swine, sheep, grains like wheat, butter, milk, sugar, salt, pepper, other spices and foodstuffs and new medicinal herbs, among many other things, to the Indians. They showed them how to make saddles and weave saddle blankets, although the Indians preferred to ride bareback. Pueblo Indians were converted to Catholicism, and they used Spanish baptismal names and were given Spanish surnames as well. Sometimes the friars Hispanicized an Indian name and had the Indians use that as their last name.

The Spanish, in turn, received cultural gifts from the Indians, including chile, tomatoes, beans, potatoes, turkey, buffalo meat and piñon nuts. They

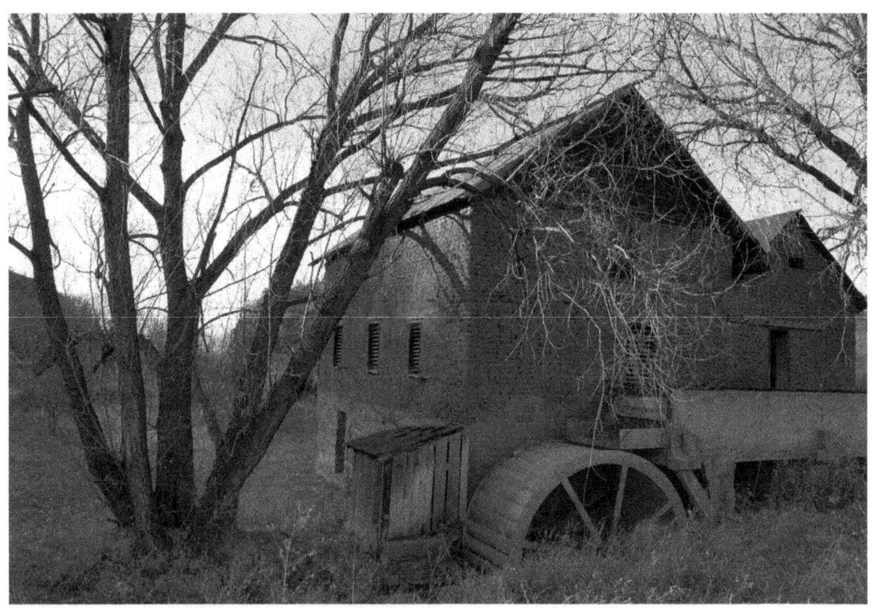

El Molino. *Photograph ©Ramón Juan Carlos de Aragón, 2011.*

also learned about sites for turquoise, various clays, medicinal plants, plants that provided roots for shampoos and flower petals for dyes. The Spanish colonists also held trade fairs in their villages throughout the territory in which the villagers from various areas gathered and traded what they grew or created. For example, those who lived near the Las Salinas Salt Lakes traveled north to trade the salt they harvested for fruits and vegetables. The settlers eventually invited friendly tribes to the trade fairs, and they traded with the Indians. Rumors that other explorers were coming to North America circulated among the missionaries and Spanish settlements.

American Colonies

On May 13, 1607, Captain John Smith established Jamestown, the first English settlement in what is now the United States, with 103 colonists. The bubonic plague came into the Americas once again, spreading from the New England colonies to Florida and Mexico.

Since San Augustine de la Florida, the present-day state of Florida (from the Spanish word for blooming, or "land of the flowers"), had been under Spain since the sixteenth century, the missionaries published a catechism in a language of Florida Indians. This book was printed in Mexíco City, the capital of New Spain, in 1612. They also published an Indian grammar book in 1614. Needless to say, Spanish friars placed great value in preserving native languages through the written word. Spanish-born missionaries evangelized the Indians in Louisiana, Florida, California, Arizona, Texas and New Mexico, where by 1639, fifty thousand converts had been counted. English settlers in New England associated Catholicism with undermining Henry VIII's Church of England.

In 1622, the Powhatan Confederacy nearly wiped out the English colony at Jamestown. Nathaniel Bacon destroyed the Paunchy in 1676, before they could lead a revolt. The Dutch colonists in New York also had their own continuous problems with the Indians. Relations with the Native Americans were often at the root of problems among the imperial powers of Spain, England, Holland, Portugal and France. More often than not, the French and English used natives as mercenaries to attack each other's settlements and those of the Spanish.

In many cases, the Indians allied with the English, Dutch and French because they trusted them, but they were always being taken advantage of. For example, Peter Minuit, a Dutch explorer, purchased Manhattan Island from the Mannahatta Indians for twenty-four dollars in trinkets. When Europeans could not trade for what they wanted, they attacked the Indians. In 1637, John Mason and a sizable English force, which included Narragansett Indians, attacked a Pequot Indian camp, killing several hundred, three hundred of whom were women and children. As a result of policies against the Indians in New England, fifty-two out of ninety English towns were attacked. Adverse policies even included a 1679 law in Virginia allowing slave owners to breed slaves to increase their labor forces. Other English laws banned all Catholics from its territories. If caught, Catholics would face imprisonment for the first offense and death for the second offense. Witchcraft was a capital crime. This also affected Indian medicine men, who were referred to as Indian witch doctors.

Great Swamp Massacre

On July 20, 1675, five years before the 1680 Pueblo Indian Revolt against the Spanish in the Southwest, several tribes, including the Pocumtue and Narragansett, joined Metacomet, leader of the Wampanoag, and Nipmuck, who called a council of war against the English colonists. Thus, the first united uprising against Europeans by Indians in North America began. The English colonists were caught completely by surprise. Several English settlements were burned to the ground, and the settlers there were killed. After this, English colonists attacked a Narragansett village, killing six hundred Indians, including women, children and twenty sachems (chiefs). This attack is known as the Great Swamp Massacre. Cononchet, the leader of the Narragansett, was captured in 1676 and killed. His body was dismembered, and his head was placed on public display. Other reprisals by the English continued furiously, and some of the tribes were wiped out, while others were nearly exterminated. Native Americans who escaped went to the Southwest, while others left for Canada. Metacomet was finally captured on August 12, 1676. His head was not only cut off but also placed on a spike in the town square of Plymouth Colony for twenty years as a memorial to the crushing of the Indian uprising by the English. In York County, colonists had the right to kill on sight any free Indian they saw in an established area. Before coming into contact with the English colonists, there were approximately forty thousand Abenakis; by 1676, they were down to only five thousand, and after the American Revolution, there were as few as one thousand.

Epidemics ravaged New Mexico, and the population of the Pueblo de Los Pecos declined dramatically. In 1640, a new epidemic hit New Mexico, and several thousand Pueblo Indians died. During this same time, Don Luis de Rosas was appointed governor, and animosity between the Apaches and the governor flared up. The Franciscans defended the Native Americans. The Spanish civil authorities and the Franciscans were constantly at odds. Drought, locusts, crop failure and disease plagued New Mexico. Both the Spanish and Indians were dying.

1680 Pueblo Revolt

A very interesting story is told that sometime in August 1680, Mary, the mother of Christ, appeared to a little ten-year-old girl named María Dolores in Santa Fé. María Dolores had a serious illness, and she was miraculously cured during the vision. The folk story goes on to relate that Mary informed the girl that the Kingdom of St. Francis (New Mexico) would go through severe hardships and suffering and would be destroyed. After the appearance, María Dolores told of her experience, and the story spread. The prophecy came true.

On August 10, 1680, the feast day of San Lorenzo, one of the most honored martyrs of the Roman Catholic Church who was reportedly burned to death on a red-hot gridiron by the Romans, the Pueblo Indians

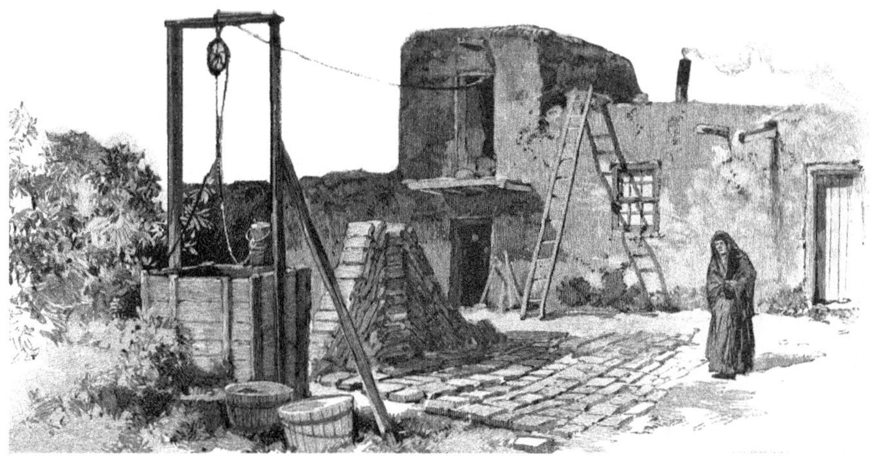

A New Mexican adobe yard, Santa Fé. Drawing. Charles Graham, *Harper's Weekly* 34, no. 1752 (July 19, 1890). *Courtesy of the author.*

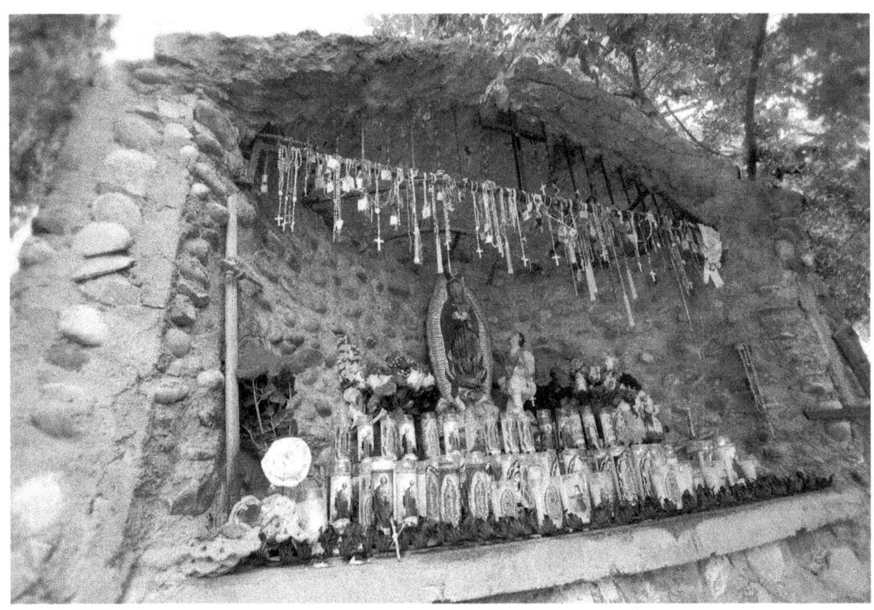

Santuario, New Mexico. *Photograph ©Ramón Juan Carlos de Aragón, 2011.*

revolted against Spanish control. It is believed the leader of the revolt was from Ohkay Owingeh, San Juan Pueblo; his name was Popé. During the uprising, the Indians massacred over four hundred Spanish men, women and children and around twenty-one friars, who were tortured and burned to death. Many of the women and girls were raped in a blood-filled frenzy. The rebellious Indians destroyed the pueblos allied with the Spanish. The churches, and any other vestiges of Spanish control, were also razed. Contrary to what has been written, not all of the pueblos united against the Spanish. Some pueblos still remained friendly with the colonists. News of the revolt reached the governor, and some of the colonists escaped, including Doña Josefa Teresa Sambrano López de Grijalva.

Doña Josefa was born in 1640 and was the dedicated *sacristana* of the Our Lady of the Assumption Church, which was built in 1626 in Santa Fé. As the sacristana, she had the duty of caring for an ancient wooden image of Mary that was brought to Santa Fé from Spain by ox cart on the El Camino Real in 1625. The capital city of Santa Fé itself was named after Santa Fé de la Granada in Spain, the scene of the surrender of Boabdil, the last Moorish sultan to King Ferdinand and Queen Isabella in 1492. This was the final act of the Reconquest of Spain from the Moors. Doña Josefa cared for a statue, which may have come from Granada. The statue is now considered to be the oldest Madonna in the United States. The nearly thirty-inch-high statue is carved from willow. An anonymous master who enriched the figure with polychrome beautifully sculpted it.

This revered image of Mary has had many titles throughout its long history, but it is most widely known as La Conquistadora de Almas, the Conqueror of Souls. Doña Josefa saved the statue. She fled with the remaining colonists south, aided by the Isleta Pueblo and other Indians to an area called El Paso del Norte, the northern river pass, meaning a cropping of the Río Grande. This site is west of the present downtown area of El Paso, Texas. It was here that the surviving colonists took refuge, and La Conquistadora was placed in safekeeping at the Nuestra Señora de Guadalupe Mission Church, which was built in 1659.

Don Diego José de Vargas Zapata y Luján Ponce de León y Contreras

In 1692, Don Diego José de Vargas Zapata y Luján Ponce de León y Contreras was able to complete the reconquest of New Mexico. De Vargas, who was later given the title of Marques de la Nava de Barcinas, led the Spanish colonists who had been in exile in El Paso back to New Mexico. He placed the statue of La Conquistadora on the end of a wooden pole and carried it as a banner, proclaiming the image to be the "Sovereign Queen, Most Blessed Mary," as he retook Santa Fé for the crown. It was believed by the Spanish that the intercession of Mary had made the reconquest possible. In 1712, an annual fiesta began in Santa Fé to honor La Conquistadora and commemorate the *Reconquista de Santa Fé*, the return of the colonists. *La Entrada*, the entry, a play portraying the entrance of de Vargas and the settlers into Santa Fé, was and continues to be reenacted.

In the past, very little has been written about the customs, diet and ways of life that the Spanish colonists introduced into New Mexico. When the settlers loaded up their wagons, they took many items they had transported all the way from their mother country, Spain. Franciscan missionaries were the trailblazers, but the colonists themselves arrived prepared to transplant their previous lives in Spain with their new lives in New Mexico. In the wagons, they carried grape vines and seeds or seedlings for apple trees, apricots, cherries and even peaches. They packed seeds for the planting of hollyhocks, which they called *varas de San José* (staffs of St. Joseph). They had flower bulbs and various colors of rose plants, which they called *Rosas*

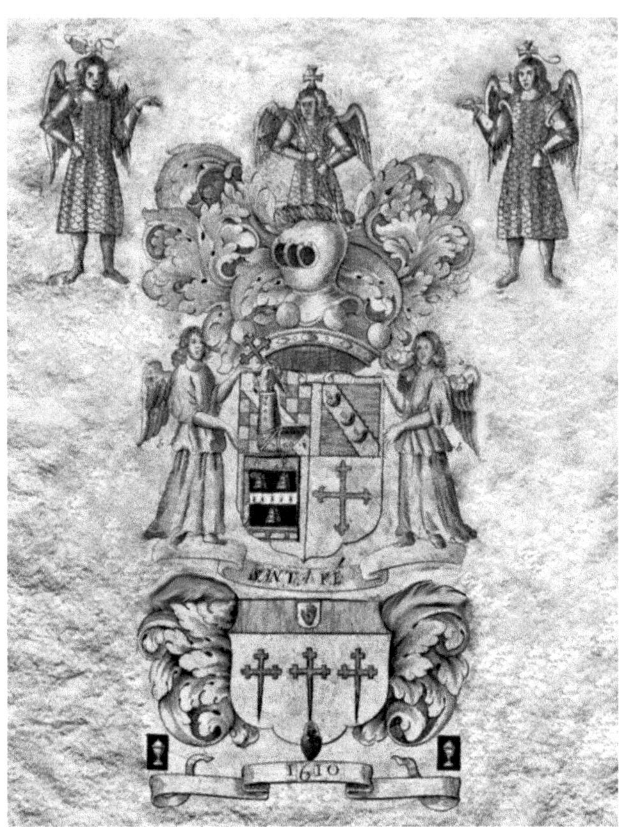

Escudo de Armas, seventeenth century. *Courtesy of the author.*

de Castilla. They also introduced spinach, beets, carrots, onions, radishes, lettuce, cucumbers, asparagus, *verdolagas* (purslane), parsnip, garlic, *habas* (peeled fava beans), melons and watermelons as crops, which they grew and cultivated in Santa Fé and the surrounding areas. Ground pepper and salt were necessities, as were sugar, rice and raisins.

They moved along flocks of chickens, goats and sheep and took herds of pigs, cattle and horses to the new farms and ranches that they established along the Río Grande, which they called "El Río de Nuestra Señora," the River of Our Lady. They took wheat for transplanting and flour, which was a staple that nourished them along the way. Tortillas (flatbread) were made with the wheat flour. The unleavened water-based dough was rolled flat and cooked on an iron grill. The white-wheat flour tortilla originated in the Mediterranean countries and was introduced into Spain by the Moors. Although similar types of flatbreads existed in other world cultures, including those of the Americas, the Indians made them from corn.

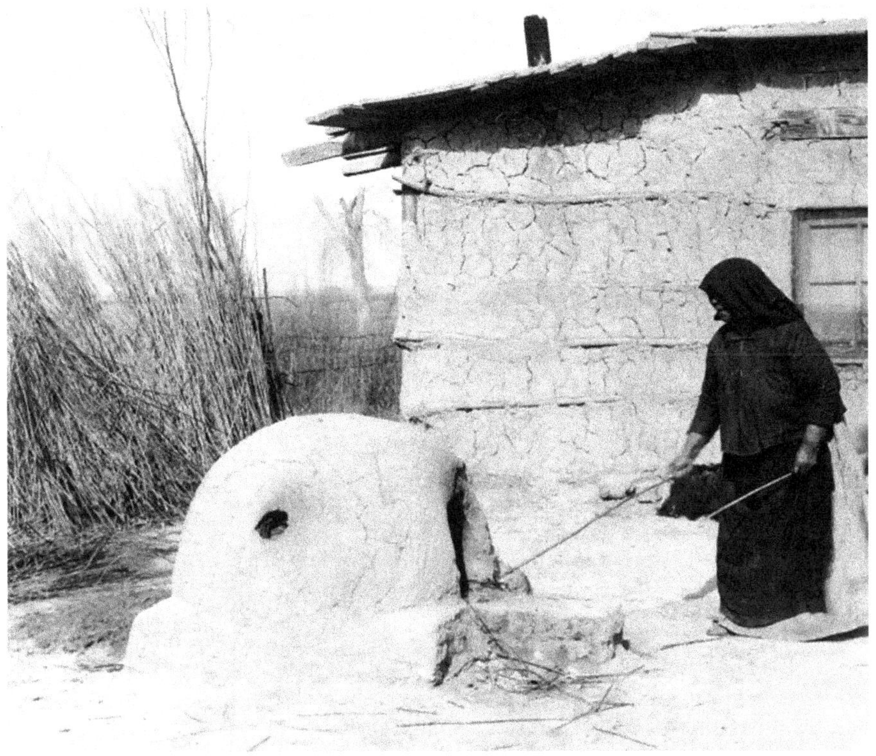

A woman baking in horno, New Mexico. Photo circa 1925, photographer unknown. *Courtesy of the author.*

The Moors also introduced the *horno*, or beehive adobe oven, into Spain for baking bread. The horno graced every single home that the Spanish settlers built. The colonists also had musical instruments, such as guitars and violins, and some of the soldiers carried military drums. Furniture items, toys for the children, games, clothing, fabric, dishes and cooking and eating utensils were also transported, along with paper and vellum, which were produced from calf, sheep, goat, pig or horse skin to write on, and ink, as well as writing implements. Weapons for protection, plants for remedies and various iron tools for construction, such as adzes, hammers and nails, were necessities to build homes in the new land. Carded wool and looms for weaving, which all of the women knew how to use, plus soaps and perfumes, were prized items. Other prized items included rosaries, prayer books, religious medals and crosses. It is a point of contention which songs the settlers sang as they journeyed along the arduous Camino Real, but they most probably sang those such as the ancient "Buenos Dias Paloma Blanca," in honor of the

Virgin Mary; "Las Mañanitas," sung on All Saints feast days; and "Bendito Sea Dios," a popular Franciscan missionary song. Hard-tack biscuits called *galletas*, cheese and beef jerky, as well as hard candy, were snacks on their journey north. The colonial settlement and resettlement eras saw continuous caravans slowly moving along the trail.

Comanche and Cuerno Verde

The Comanche tribe dominated large areas in West Texas, New Mexico and northern Coahuila in Mexico. The Comanche were a powerful tribe that became expert horsemen. The New Mexico governor, Juan Bautista de Anza, with six hundred Spanish soldiers and Indian warriors, fought against the Comanche and defeated Cuerno Verde (Green Horn), their leader. The Comanche and the governor were finally able to come to a compromise, and a treaty was signed. The Comanche traded with the Comancheros and hunted with the Ciboleros. Comancheros were a group of fearless Spanish men whom the Comanche admired and respected. Los Ciboleros (buffalo hunters) were also Spanish men from the villages who provided a necessary service for the survival of the communities. They hunted bison and returned with large quantities of meat, hides, horns and other items the villagers needed. With the arrival of the American cavalry in the southern plains, the Comanche were finally subdued and forced to live on reservations.

Apache and Mangas Coloradas

Apache leader Mangas Coloradas signed a peace treaty in 1846 with the United States. The soldiers were granted safe passage through the lands occupied by the Apache in exchange for peace and not being moved from their land. Mangas Coloradas kept his part of the treaty, but a group of miners attacked him and left him tied to a tree. The Apache then went into a full-fledged war against the Americans. Brigadier General Joseph Rodman West and his troops succeeded in capturing the Apache chief. Historian Edwin R. Sweeney wrote:

> *The Americans killed four Indians, wounded others, and captured thirteen women and children. Mangas Coloradas entered the Fort under a white flag of truce. West ordered armed soldiers to take him into custody and*

ordered that Mangas Coloradas be executed after being tortured. After killing Mangas Coloradas, the general ordered that the Apache's head be cut off, boiled, and sent to the Smithsonian Institution. The mutilation of Mangas' body angered his tribe and hostilities between the U.S. and Apaches increased. The Apaches were forced to surrender in 1886 when they were captured and those who lived were deported to Florida and Alabama where they suffered military imprisonment.

The Mescalero Apache were held at Fort Sumner without clean water or firewood for cooking. Many of the Native Americans died from severe illness and hunger.

Crazy Horse

Crazy Horse was born into the Ogalala band of the Lakota (Sioux) Nation near the Black Hills of South Dakota in 1840. He was a great leader and powerful warrior. He was well liked and admired by almost everyone who knew him. He was devastated when his brother, Little Hawk, was killed. Crazy Horse loved his people and valued their freedom so much that he fought for many years to defend it. He made many treaties with the United States government, but each one of these treaties would be broken. Native land was being taken away, and his people were dying. In 1877, he finally surrendered because the United States promised his people would get their own reservation in the north near the Powder River. As he and his people struggled to survive where they lived near Fort Robinson, he continuously reminded the U.S. government of the promise it had made. During one of these discussions, Crazy Horse was arrested. He tried to get free because he couldn't stand the thought of being imprisoned. A soldier stabbed him in the back, and he died on September 5, 1877, at the age of about thirty-five.

Chief Joseph

Hin-mah-too-yah-lat-kekt, or Chief Joseph, was born on March 3, 1840, in Wallowa Valley, Oregon. He became the leader of the Wal-lam-wat-kain (Wallowa) band of Nez Perce. He made a treaty with the U.S. government, and he and his people were put on a reservation. Four years later, the government threatened war if they did not agree to move to a smaller reservation in

Idaho. They did not want to leave their native land. The United States sent two thousand soldiers, led by General Howard, to pursue and kill the eight hundred Nez Perce who would not move. For three months, the Nez Perce outmaneuvered and battled their pursuers, traveling 1,170 miles. Finally, just 40 miles from Canada, after a devastating five-day battle in freezing temperatures and with no food, Chief Joseph surrendered. He said:

> *Tell General Howard I know his heart. What he told me before; I have it in my heart. I am tired of fighting. Our chiefs are killed; Looking Glass is dead, Too-hul-hul-sote is dead. The old men are all dead. It is the young men who say yes or no. He who led on the young men is dead. It is cold, and we have no blankets; the little children are freezing to death. My people, some of them, have run away to the hills, and have no blankets, no food. No one knows where they are—perhaps freezing to death. I want to have time to look for my children, and see how many of them I can find. Maybe I shall find them among the dead. Hear me, my chiefs! I am tired; my heart is sick and sad. From where the sun now stands, I will fight no more forever.*

A treaty Chief Joseph signed was worthless. General William Sherman forced Chief Joseph and four hundred of his followers to be taken to a prisoner of war camp. The surviving Nez Perce were taken by rail to a reservation in Oklahoma for seven years. Many of them died. Chief Joseph continued to plead for his people. In 1879, Chief Joseph met with President Rutherford B. Hayes, and finally in 1885, some of his people were allowed to return to a small reservation on their homeland, but Chief Joseph was taken away from his people and sent to Colville Indian Reservation in Idaho. Joseph continued to plead his case, meeting with President Ulysses Grant, and in 1903 he visited President Theodore Roosevelt in Washington. Until his death in 1904, he continued to speak "eloquently" against the injustice of the United States' policy toward his people and hoped someday America's "promise of freedom and equality might one day be fulfilled for Native American as well."

LONG WALK

The Navajo, likely from the Spanish word *navaja*, meaning "knife," who call themselves *Dineh*, the "People," were the largest tribe in North America. This Nomadic tribe eventually became self-sufficient with the skills they learned from the Spanish, including farming, herding sheep and weaving. They also became well known as silversmiths, continuing the designs and traditions in their woven rugs and silver jewelry that had been introduced to them by the Spanish colonists. They learned the use of the horno, brought to New Mexico by the Spanish and which the Spanish in turn had learned to build from the Moors. Brigadier General James H. Carlton in New Mexico turned his attention to the Navajos, numbering around 300,000. They controlled over sixteen million acres of land in the territory of New Mexico, which included Arizona and land in Utah. The chief Narbonne was killed in 1849, so hostilities between the Navajo and Americans increased. This culminated with the "Long Walk" in 1863, meant to uproot and relocate them. By then, only 8,000 survived in the dead of winter without shoes, food, water, blankets or appropriate clothing to withstand the cold. The Navajos were forcibly relocated by the U.S. military under the command of Christopher "Kit" Carson. Under the American government, they were forced to live through domination, subjugation, starvation and severe exposure to the elements on a reservation nearly three hundred miles

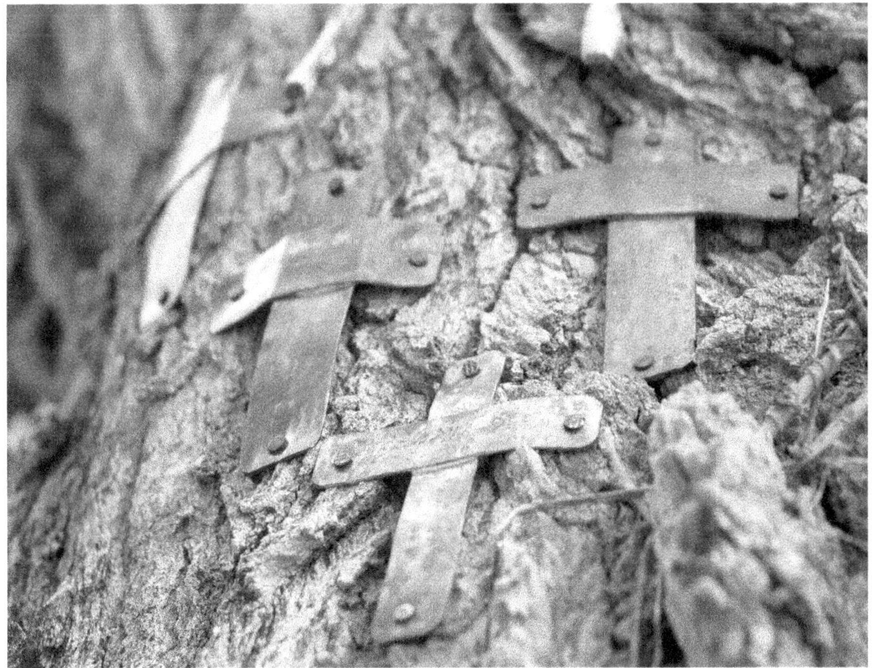

Cruzes. *Photograph ©Ramón Juan Carlos de Aragón, 2011.*

from their homeland. In 1970, the United Native American tribes declared Thanksgiving Day as the "National Day of Mourning" for the Indians in the United States.

According to C.F. Lummis in his book titled *The Spanish Pioneers*:

> *The legislation of Spain in behalf of the Indians everywhere was incomparably more extensive, more comprehensive, more systematic and more humane than that of Great Britain, the Colonies and the present United States combined...There have been Spanish schools for Indians in America since 1524. By 1575—nearly a century before there was a printing-press in English America—many books in twelve different Indian languages had been printed in the city of Mexico, whereas in our history John Eliot's Indian Bible stands alone; and three Spanish universities in America were nearly rounding out their century when Harvard was founded. A surprisingly large proportion of the pioneers of southwestern America were college men; and intelligence went hand in hand with heroism in the early settlement of the New World.*

FRAY FRANCISCO JUAN DE PADILLA: NEW MEXICO'S FAMOUS MARTYR

When the Spanish came to the New World, saintly apparitions were said to be taking place everywhere throughout the Spanish Empire. The appearances of Our Lady of Guadalupe in Mexico in 1533 are the most well known. The highly prized possessions of the people included religious medals, hand-wrought painted images of Christ and the saints and *relicarios*, which were reliquaries that contained relics of the saints. The relics were tiny fragments of the bones of the saints or bits of their actual clothing. Anything that was associated with the saints was highly valued, and miraculous cures were attributed to them. A mystery took place in one of the Indian Pueblos of New Mexico, which involved many of the spiritual beliefs that had been handed down for generations among the Spanish colonists.

It was a very beautiful Christmas Eve at the venerable Pueblo of Isleta on December 24, 1889. Father Andrew Eschalier, the parish priest, went rushing around in the ancient church of San Antonio de Padua, which was renamed San Augustine, making final preparations for the Mass that was to be held at midnight. The priest decided to return to the rectory, have dinner and make ready for the Mass. Father Eschalier had no idea that the village

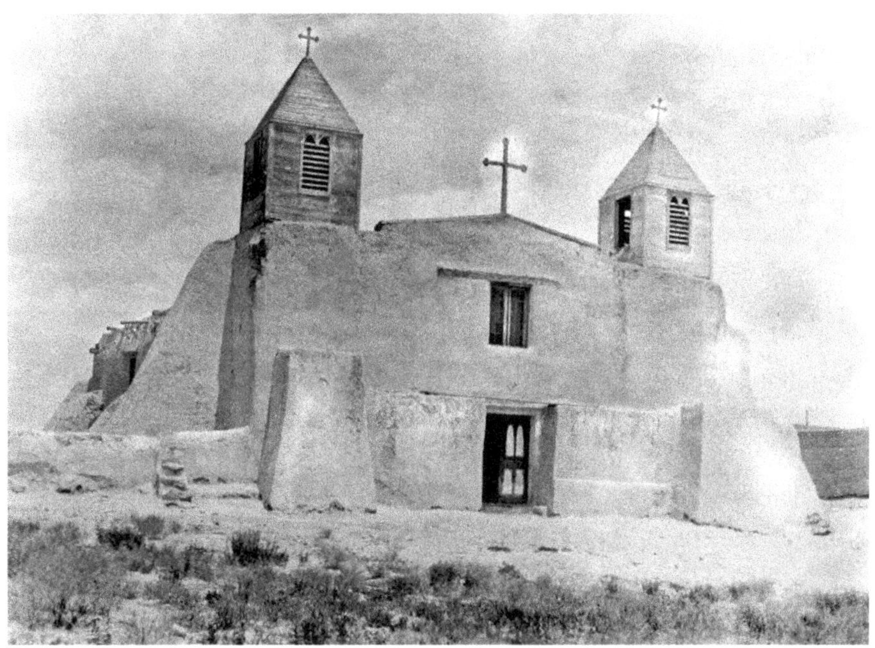

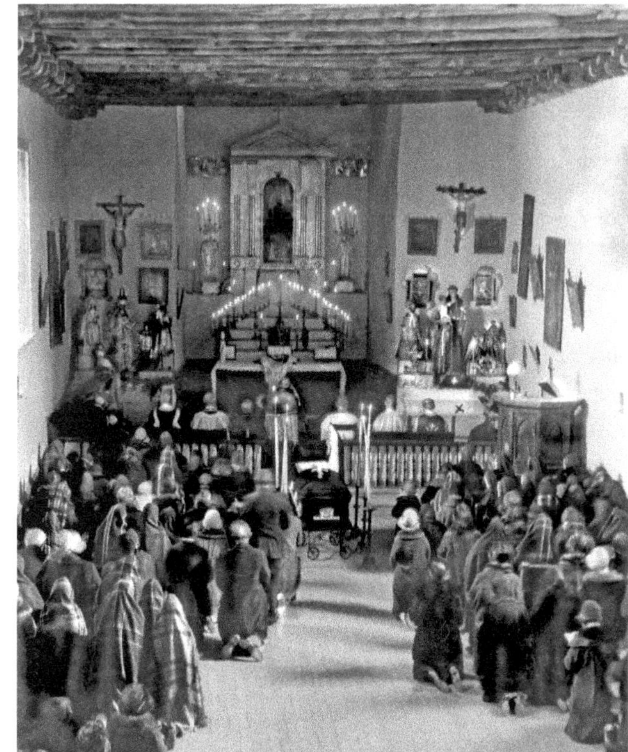

Above: San Augustine Church. Charles Lummis, circa 1880. *Courtesy of the author.*

Right: Funeral of Father Anton Docher of Isleta Pueblo. Photo December 18, 1928, photographer unknown. *Courtesy of Philippe Morvan.*

elders had decided to perform a ceremonial dance within the walls of the church before the Mass.

At about eight o'clock that night, lit luminaries of crisscrossed piles of piñon and sabino wood logs burned brightly in front of the church in the night sky. The native dancers filed in as the flames cast their shadows on the exterior walls. Excitement filled the air as the Indians gathered and began to dance on the wood planks that covered the floor to the beat of the drums and rattles.

The San Antonio Church built in 1613 had withstood the destructive force of the Pueblo Indian Rebellion of 1680. The Indians of Isleta had sided with the Spanish, as did some of the other Pueblo Indian tribes. The fate that befell the various loyal pueblos who allied with the Spanish was that Popé and his rebellious warriors destroyed them in a mad frenzy of murder, rape and pillage. The exodus of the surviving Spaniards to an area called El Paso del Norte included the Isleta Indians, who left the territory with them in fear of reprisal. When the Spanish Reconquest of 1692 took place under General and Governor Don Diego de Vargas, most of the Isletans returned to their ancestral pueblo. The Indians who stayed behind founded the Pueblo of Isleta Del Sur near El Paso, Texas. Upon returning to Isleta, the Indians and Spanish found that the interior of the church and the roof had been burned. It was rebuilt in 1719.

On Christmas Eve 1889, the Isletans performed a traditional dance in the church that had been passed down in their tribe for generations. The male dancers painted the left sides of their bodies one color and the right sides another. The women painted their cheeks red and wore *tablitas*, painted boards, on their heads. The men tied macaw feathers in their hair, and they all danced barefoot. While dancing in the body of the church, the Indians were dressed in their colorful regalia, at first dancing lightly and then increasing their tempo to the faster beat of the drums. Suddenly, a creaking noise on the floor near the altar was heard. The dancers continued, even though the strange noise became as loud as the singing and the thundering footsteps on the wood floor. Loud banging and then dull heavy sounds, like those coming from a hard object striking the surface, could be heard. María Marcelina Lucero, an eyewitness, described the noise as that of someone "kicking on the floor." Since the frightening sound could no longer be ignored, the dancers stopped, and all of the Indians stared overwhelmed with wonder toward the altar. Then the floorboards started popping up on the Gospel side of the sanctuary, and suddenly, to the amazement of all who were watching, the altar mysteriously moved.

The Indians ran out of the church terrified. In their bewilderment, they talked outside the church in their native tongue about what they had just seen. Pablo Abeyta, one of the Indians who had been standing near the entry between the railings to the sanctuary, led a group to check the altar. The sound had stopped, and they wondered if someone was responsible for what had happened. After examining everything, they found no one hiding who could have been responsible for what had taken place. Father Eschalier was informed about the strange occurrence. Although he tried to quiet down the anxiety in the pueblo and go on with the normal day-to-day activities of the church, news about the mystery spread out to the nearby Spanish villages, including those of Los Padillas, Peralta and Valencia. When it was finally decided to check under the floor near the altar, they found a hand-hewn coffin made from a hollowed-out cottonwood tree lying directly under the boards. A cottonwood lid was removed, and the mummified body of a Spanish friar came into view. This was not the first time that the miracle of the rising coffin of Fray Francisco Juan de Padilla at San Augustine de la Isleta had taken place.

Around 1850, at about the time of the arrival of the controversial Bishop Jean Baptiste Lamy in New Mexico, the coffin rose from the depths of the earth and appeared above the ground. Juan Andres Zuni, an Isleta Indian, claimed he saw the coffin opened and that he and others looked at the body of the priest Juan Francisco Padilla. Along with Zuni, José Chiwiwi, another Indian of the village, said that the fray's body was complete and unmarred by any decay. Marcelina Lucero de Abeyta, as a little girl, also saw the fray after he "rose above the earth." The coffin was reburied several feet into the ground, and a wood floor was installed shortly after the appearance to keep it from rising to the surface. People at Isleta knew that the coffin containing the remains of the "Holy Priest" had risen up through several feet of soil many times after it was first buried by the altar, but no one knew exactly how often this had happened. Legend has it that it went as far back as the seventeenth century. Some of the Indians also knew that other coffins of the deceased that were buried in the floors of the church and altar—a common practice during the Spanish colonial and Mexican periods of New Mexico—and those buried in the immediate area outside the church did not rise from the earth as this one did. What was so special or unusual about this one?

In the month of July in the year 1819, the coffin arose. The Reverend Father Fray Juan Francisco de Hocio, who was the vicar prelate of New Mexico under the archbishopric of Durango in New Spain, arrived in Isleta. He got to Isleta after a two-day journey from Santa Fé on July 5, 1819.

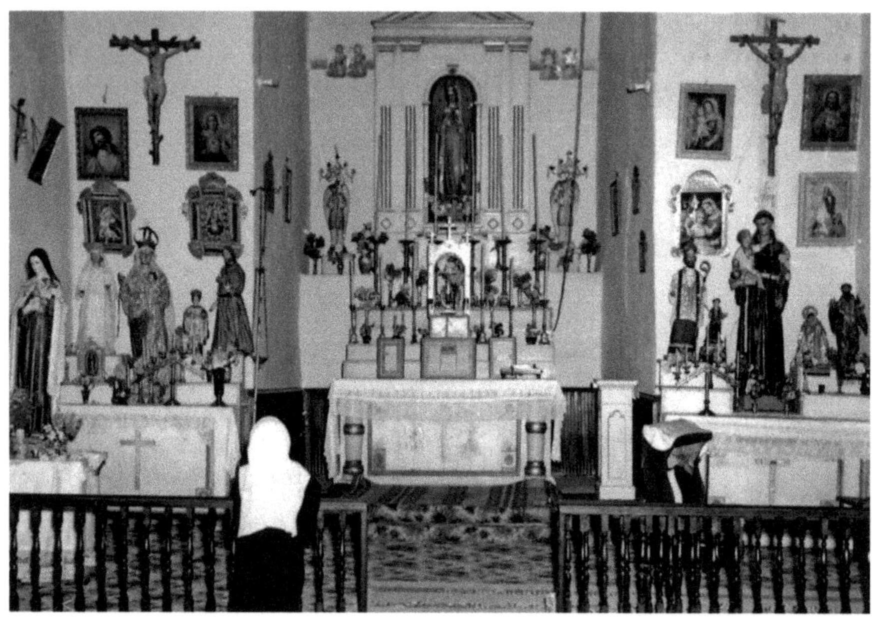

Isleta Church altar. Photo circa 1950, photographer unknown. *Courtesy of the author.*

Immediately after his arrival for his juridical visitations to New Mexico's parishes and missions, Fray de Hocio was informed by the pastor of San Agustín de la Isleta and its mission churches of San José de la Laguna and la Inmaculada de la Concepción de Tomé about a rising coffin. This priest, Fray Ignacio Sánchez, was stunned by a coffin that apparently "gradually has been coming up from the depth at which it was buried, until it reached the surface of the floor, at the Gospel side of the sanctuary of the church." Interestingly, Fray Sánchez was confused as to whose body was in the coffin. However, Fray de Hocio observed, "In effect, having examined the grave, I noticed that the coffin was becoming visible, therefore I ordered that on the next day, on the 6th of July, the coffin should be taken out, and this was done between 8:00 and 9:00 in the morning in my presence, and that of my secretary, Fray Andres Correa." Three other priests were accompanying Fray de Hocio and his entourage, which included five distinguished laymen of the area, one of whom, Don Francisco Xavier Chávez, became the first governor of New Mexico under the Mexican Republic.

After the casket was uncovered, Fray de Hocio and Fray Correa took the body, which was incorruptible, out of the coffin and placed it on a table in the middle of the church. The indigo-blue homespun habit on the body crumbled to pieces as they moved it. The friar's blue habit represented the blue mantle of Mary, the mother of Christ, and signified the virtues of poverty, chastity and obedience. Spanish Franciscans serving in the missions of Nueva España during the colonial period were conceded the privilege of wearing blue habits in honor of the Virgin Mary. They could also wear blue vestments and stoles on her feast days. They wore leather sandals and knotted cord girdles. Around the neck of the body was a rosary with a centerpiece medal embossed with the images of San Francisco de Asís and San Juan Nepomuceno, the patrons and namesakes of the fray whose body was in the coffin. The custom of the religious order of monks and cloistered nuns from antiquity was to adopt the names of patron saints and to dedicate their lives and works to these saints. *Escudos de Monja*, which were nun's badges with painted or engraved religious images, were used by the women, and the men used adorned medals or pendants called *relicarios* with actual relics of the saints (bits of bone, teeth or scraps of cloth). Fray de Hocio found a relicario on the body "of a heavenly blue, so bright as if it had just been unrolled from the bolt." From whom did this heavenly bright blue piece of cloth come? It was clearly obvious that the fray in the coffin had dedicated his priesthood to Saint Francis and Saint John, and he took the names of the two saints for his ordination.

As the body was cleansed, the five priests and the five laymen noticed a very pleasant perfume-like aroma coming from the corpse. Observing the body, they all determined by its appearance that the man had been around thirty to thirty-six years of age when he died. In the coffin, the astounded priests found a disintegrating paper with parts of the date June 4, 177(?). This day was noted on the fragments as the date of the second time the coffin was buried after it had arisen from its deep burial place to the surface of the ground. At this time, elders of the Isleta Pueblo said that the body of the fray had been buried in the ground of the church thirty-two years earlier and that they believed it had been forty-four years before the body was placed in the cottonwood coffin. This would bring the date to about 1694, which could have been the date the body was taken to the church at Isleta for burial.

According to oral tradition at the pueblo of Isleta, the body was that of Fray Francisco Juan de Padilla, although they called him Fray Juan Francisco Padilla. Fray de Padilla, along with Fray Juan de la Cruz and Fray Luis de Escalona, arrived in New Mexico in 1540 with the Francisco Vásquez de Coronado Expedition. The three priests stayed in New Mexico to minister among the Indians when Coronado and his party returned to New Spain.

Fray de Padilla was the youngest of the three priests. The other two men were much older. Fray Francisco Juan de Padilla was born in Andalucía, Spain. He had been a soldier before joining the Franciscan Order of Friars Minor. About 1528, he arrived in New Spain, where he became a member of the Franciscan province of the Holy Gospel. His arrival in the city of Mexico placed him in the area around the time of the miraculous appearances of Our Lady of Guadalupe. De Padilla vehemently sought to prevent the oppression of the Indians. He founded the convent of Tzapotlan, where he became its first superior. He then founded another convent at Tuchpan and made it the headquarters for the missionary friars. De Padilla founded a convent in Jalisco and then finally established a monastery, which he governed until 1540, when he traveled with Coronado to New Mexico.

While in Mexico, Fray Francisco Juan de Padilla evangelized and converted countless Indians. In New Mexico, he ministered in the Tiquex province of pueblos located along the banks of the Río Grande, which was first called the Río de Nuestra Señora, or River of Our Lady, in honor of Mary, the mother of Christ. Fray de Padilla was noted for his use of Spanish and Latin liturgical songs, music and religious art in his conversion of the Indians. The priests set out on an apostolate journey along with the *novicios*, the novitiates, Tarascan Indians from Mexico being trained for the priesthood, dressed in knee-length gray tunics and girded with the knotted cord of the Franciscans; various servants, including a black and a *mulato*; and a Portuguese soldier named Andres de Campo. Coronado gave the missionary group aid up until they arrived in Cicuye (Pecos) with sheep, mules, native Indian guides and various gifts for those they would encounter. Fray Luis stayed in Cicuye. Fray Juan de la Cruz headed in another direction, and Fray de Padilla, along with a group of Cicuye Indians, the Tarascan novitiates, the black man, the *mulato* and the Portuguese soldier, headed for Quivira, an area on the eastern plains. Fray Francisco Juan de Padilla ministered for about two years converting the Indians of Quivira, and then after a string of successful conversions, he headed toward the Salinas country of New Mexico in an attempt to win more souls.

After a few days' journey on November 30, 1544, Fray de Padilla's large party of Jumano Indians, his novitiates Lucas and Sebastian, the black and *mulato*, the Portuguese soldier and various members of other tribes, including Cicuye Indians from Pecos, were surrounded by a war party of Plains Indians. Fray de Padilla ordered the soldier and others to try to escape while he walked alone, dressed in his blue habit with a knotted cord girdle and leather sandals, into their midst. The intention of the marauding Indians was clearly visible.

They were intent on stealing their goods and provisions. Fray Francisco Juan de Padilla was not moved. He knelt down, embracing a cross that he carried, and awaited his destiny in prayer and forgiveness for those who would harm him. One of the warriors rushed toward him and struck him with a stone axe on the side of the head below his left ear. As the death-dealing blow was given, it was said that storm clouds gathered in the sky, and thunder and lightning menaced the land. In fear, the attacking Indians picked up the body and threw it into a nearby natural cavity in the ground, piling rocks on top of it in hopes of containing the priest's perceived powers.

After the war party left, the others who had sought refuge removed the stones and retrieved the body. Instead of burying it, they took it to a cave and hid it. At the time of the priest's death, the two young Indians studying for the priesthood, Lucas and Sebastian, were with him. They were permitted to bury him and most probably hollowed out the cottonwood coffin to a depth of sixteen inches and a width of seventeen inches, which showed that the fray was a small and thin man. After Lucas and Sebastian returned to Mexico, it is interesting to note that Lucas returned to New Mexico as an ordained missionary priest. One could conjecture that he returned for Fray de Padilla's body to provide it with a proper burial. As the years passed, those Indians and their descendants would return to the cave and marvel at seeing the body of this holy man that would not decay. At long last, before or about 1694, the Indians, with the body of Fray Francisco Juan de Padilla in its coffin made from a hollowed-out cottonwood log, traveled for many miles in a solemn procession to the church at Isleta Pueblo. Here the coffin was buried near the altar and would rise up through the dirt with the restless body of the saintly priest.

On the night of July 6, 1819, the priests dressed the body with a new habit. They held an all-night vigil, praying for the repose of the soul. On the morning of the seventh, all of the priests held a solemn Mass, during which they sang "with the office of the dead with common responsorial and corresponding tolling of the bells." Fray de Hocio ordered that the coffin be buried in the ground with an inscription that incorrectly identified the remains as those of Fray Juan José Padilla, "a religious priest, who was minister of the mission of San Jose de la Laguna." In one fell swoop, Fray de Hocio unknowingly discounted the artifacts in the coffin and the generations-old tradition that the remains were those of Fray Francisco Juan de Padilla of the Coronado expedition. Later on, documents revealed that the Fray Juan José Padilla to whom Fray José Ignacio Sánchez and Fray Juan Francisco de Hocio alluded as a Franciscan missionary murdered in 1743

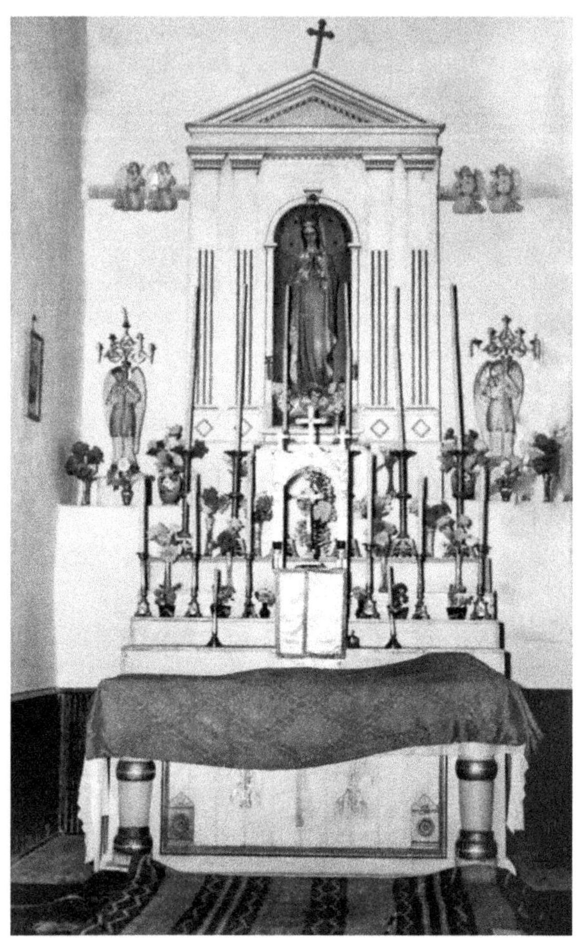

Isleta Church altar. Photo circa 1950, photographer unknown. *Courtesy of the author.*

was still signing baptism and death registers at the Isleta Church through the year 1755. Records reveal that he died peacefully of old age.

Six years after the rising of the coffin of Fray Francisco Juan de Padilla at Isleta Pueblo in 1889, Archbishop Louis Placide Chappelle ordered an investigation. His predecessor, Archbishop Jean Baptiste Salpointe, had chosen to disregard the entire event. However, from the time of the coffin's rising in 1889, Father Eschalier had been reassigned, and Father Anton Docher had taken over. Father Docher considered what was happening a mystical miracle from God. He especially took into account that when the body of the fray was exposed, the Indians from Isleta and Hispanos were taking bits of cloth and any relic that could be removed. These individuals claimed that numerous miracles could be attributed to these relics and that the holy spirit of the fray was appearing at night, helping all those who were in need. Men, women and children traveled by the hundreds to see the body, and it was claimed in the official report that they were inspired with reverence "by what they saw." The Indians believed the fray's body could levitate in the coffin and push it through the ground until it would reach the surface to perform miracles. A tinsmith, later on called the Isleta Tinsmith, was inspired by the incidents at Isleta, and he began producing religious images for devotion, including some with relics. But it wasn't until Father Docher claimed he had gotten an inexplicable infection in his hand and arm and it had turned black that the archbishop paid attention. Doctors told Father Docher that his arm had gangrene and had to be amputated. The priest knelt before the coffin of de Padilla and promised a novena of prayers—a succession of devotions for nine days each year—if he should be cured. Father Anton Docher was cured completely. Archbishop Chappelle ordered an investigation.

The investigation took place on April 25, 1895, at nine o'clock in the morning. Nine priests took part, including the pastors of Bernalillo, Las Vegas, Albuquerque, Socorro, Belen, Tiptonville and Isleta. Reverend James H. Defouri from the Our Lady of Sorrows Parish in Las Vegas was the promoter, which meant he was in charge of promoting the cause for the fray's sainthood. Reverend Juan Benito Brun of Socorro was the lawyer against the promotion of the fray. The sexton of the Isleta parish was included, along with three other employees of the church. The territorial governor of New Mexico, William T. Thornton, appointed Dr. Ruben Tipton to represent the government in the investigation. Dr. Tipton was the medical superintendent of the territorial insane asylum in Las Vegas. Dr. Tipton had a reputation as the most knowledgeable medical expert on crime scene investigation and human remains analysis. From the very outset, the committee of specialists looked at the body as being the remains of "Reverend Francisco Padilla, who had been killed by the Indians of Quivira, according to tradition three hundred years before." The date of the fray's death, according to oral history, would have been 1545.

Reverend José Maria Coudert, chairman of the proceedings, recorded, "Before our eyes the boards of the floor were lifted and the supposed body of the deceased Fray Francisco Padilla was found in the very site where by local tradition he was known to have been buried." The coffin was described as a hollowed-out cottonwood tree measuring six feet by seven inches, with a width of seventeen inches and a depth of sixteen inches. The diminutive fray's measurement was five feet. He had a purple stole around his neck.

Purple is the color priests would wear at Christmas and Lent. Diego Abeyta, who had served as the sexton of the church for a period of sixty-four years, informed the committee that, according to ancient tradition, the coffin of Fray de Padilla rose up "just prior to the time that the Indians persecuted the Spaniards." This would place the date to a little before 1680, which was the date of the Pueblo Indian Revolt. The fray was holding a book in his hands. The commission failed to say what the book was. It might be appropriate to add that the book disappeared, but no one knew when. A hood or cowl, to which the investigative team referred as "a bonnet," was also found.

Dr. Tipton corroborated in his report that the friar's left foot was missing, as were the toes of the right foot. These parts were no doubt taken at some point in time as miraculous relics. A wound was found under the left ear, which was determined to be the cause of death. However, the eyes and tongue had been torn out, which quite possibly indicated that this was done at the time of his death. The Indians, like other ancient cultures, believed that by taking out the eyes and tongue the spirit of the person was removed and therefore could not come back with the ability to see and speak. This was done to someone who was especially feared. It was also believed by some tribes of Indians that by taking some body parts from a person, that person's powers or abilities could be transferred to another.

The group concluded that there was no scientific explanation as to how the coffin could rise up through several feet of dirt to the surface. A possible reason that was finally dismissed was that the water level underground in some inexplicable way always pushed the coffin up. However, it was pointed out that the church sits on a rise, and the ground slopes down gradually toward the river, which is several hundreds of feet away. It was also taken into account that the coffin has risen up during periods of severe drought and that other coffins buried in the church and grounds do not rise up. The findings of the investigative committee were sealed in a steel box and placed in the coffin. One story goes that the original coffin was exchanged for a new, heavier oak one. Documents commemorating the life of Fray Francisco Juan de Padilla and the miracles at the Isleta Church were framed and placed on the altar. This was a common practice in the churches of Europe and in those in the Americas with documented miracles. A copy of the report was sent to the pope in Rome. The case was closed—or was it?

During the 1950s, persistent drought plagued New Mexico. This was the worst period of drought affecting the state in the twentieth century, and it lasted into the 1960s. During this time, the vast pinto bean production, which had been the major export for New Mexico for decades, ground to a halt. "Dry land" bean farming, which had peaked during World War II, came to an abrupt end. In fact, strict water rationing was in place in Albuquerque. Nearby communities like Isleta Pueblo were severely impacted by the lack of water. The coffin of Fray Francisco Juan de Padilla rose up once again. The archbishop of Santa Fé, James Peter Davis, was notified, and the rising once again caused a widespread sensation. The story received media attention. This time, however, church officials had no comment. The coffin was reburied at the altar. But everyone wonders, "Is the fray's body still rising?"

Doña Teresa de Aguilera y Roche

Doña Teresa held her head up high as she was led with bound wrists before the Holy Inquisition. A black-robed and hooded inquisitor solemnly read the serious charges against her. In New Spain, the Inquisition was a tribunal of church clerics empowered to seek out those accused of witchcraft and heresy. They held lengthy trials but dispensed justice swiftly. Doña Teresa faced up to her accusers and stated her case.

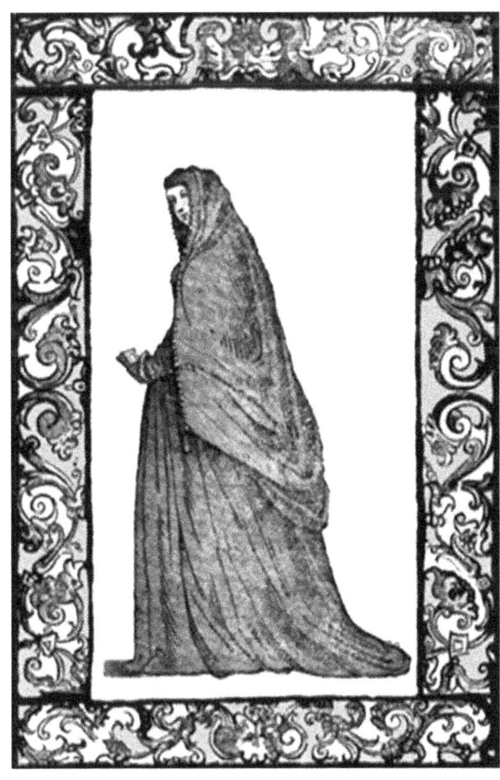

A dress for widows. Cesare Vecellio woodcut, circa 1598. *Courtesy of the author.*

In 1659, Bernardo López de Mendizabal and his wife, Doña Teresa de Aguilera y Roche, arrived in the Spanish colonial Villa of Santa Fé. He was the new provincial governor appointed by the viceroy, the Duke of Alburquerque. The forty-year-old governor was a native of the province of Chietla in New Spain. His noble ancestors held positions of distinction in the service of the Spanish crown. After spending several years in the galleon service, López went to Cartagena, where his cousin was a bishop. It was there that he met and married Doña Teresa. Teresa's mother was an Irish Catholic who had moved to Spain from Britain to escape religious persecution. Teresa herself was born in Alexandria, Italy, and she was reared in the household of the Marques de Santa Cruz. Her father, Don Melchor de Aguilera, served as governor of Cartagena de las Indias at the time of her marriage to Don Bernardo.

The Villa de Santa Fé was a relatively new settlement, founded in 1610 as the capital of New Mexico. The government at Santa Fé had experienced periods of relative peace with the Indians, interspersed with rivalries between church officials and government leaders. The Franciscan priests kept a close watch on the civil government headquartered at the Palace of the Governors. The battles between the civil leaders at Santa Fé and the Franciscan friars, with their main center at Santo Domingo Pueblo, were beyond belief. On a dark and gloomy day in 1613, a bitter feud between Governor Don Pedro de Peralta and the Franciscan superior, Father Ordoñez, ended in tragedy. The enraged governor took pot shots with a pistol at the scampering priest. Governor Peralta missed the target but hit two innocent bystanders and wounded them. The civil and religious rift in New Mexico grew even deeper with the arrival of López.

Governor Bernardo López de Mendizabal began his tenure in office with many problems. The fact that he was an advocate of the supremacy of secular over religious authority did not help matters much. Mendizabal and his young wife soon became the talk of the town. They leveled gossip about her reading out loud from a strange black book in a most peculiar tongue. She laughed to herself while reading it, and she appeared to converse with someone who was invisible, a servant told others. The servant who circulated the story was suspicious concerning the character of this mysterious book.

The rumors multiplied. It was shocking. The peculiar couple was accused of washing their hair and bathing on Friday nights. This forbidden activity was clearly a Jewish rite, which was anti-Christian. They even preferred to sleep in separate bedrooms. This custom in itself was scandalous in seventeenth-century New Mexico. Doña Teresa was also accustomed to primping on Saturday, as if celebrating that day "which the dead law of Moses ordered to be observed." She was accused of giving her husband "powders" to make herself more desirable to him. Doña Teresa even used the peels of onions on the soles of her feet.

Along with the implications concerning the guilt of promoting Judaism came the charge that the couple failed to fulfill their Christian religious obligations. The servants were also never permitted to enter their bedrooms with them. Governor López and Doña Teresa were both reported to the

Inquisition. As if this were not enough, many of the governor's policies were unpopular and brought him into continuous conflict with the Franciscans, as well as the local citizens.

After his arrival, Governor López raised the wages Indians received for their labor as farmers and herdsmen for the colonists from half a real a day to a full real per day, plus food. On the surface, it was a commendable act, but the end result was that the colonists could not afford the new rate and were forced to go without hiring the Indian laborers. The friars were also deprived of herdsmen and servants through an order given by the governor. However, López made use of the unemployed Indians by having them work for him, but he never made full payment for their services and was accused of exploiting Indian labor for his own self-interests. The governor seized the palm mats that the Indians of Sevilleta Pueblo used as beds and confiscated the hides they used to manufacture sandals. Many of the Indians he pressed into service in the salt fields became ill due to the heavy labor and maltreatment they received from their overseers.

It was claimed that the new governor displayed such arrogance and an uncompromising attitude toward the people and their religious leaders that

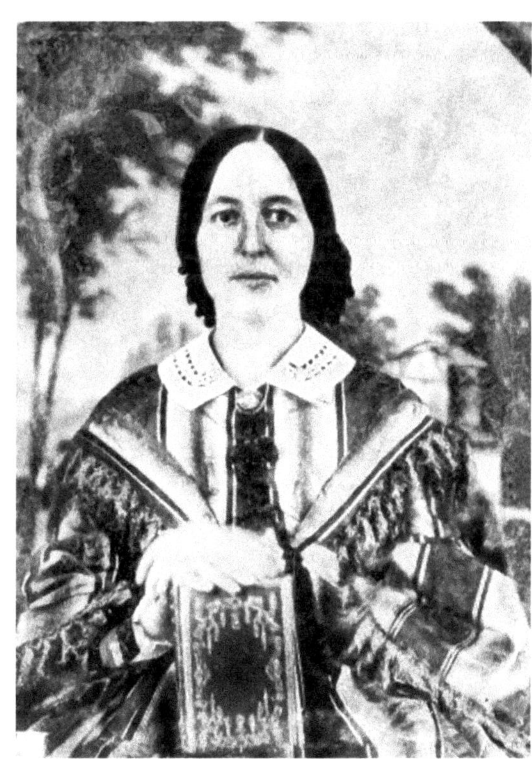

María Ignacia Jaramillo. Ambrotype, Taos. Photographer and date unknown. *Courtesy of the author.*

he incurred the dislike of most everyone. He asked the women to embroider doublets and shirts for him, and if they refused, he threatened to give them two hundred lashes and imprison them in the Casa Real, where he would "keep them spinning and embroidering all day." It was rumored that Doña Teresa was only content with her privacy. She did occasionally receive gifts from her husband, which were actually bribes he had accepted (about which she knew nothing). In reality, Doña Teresa was not a particularly greedy person, nor was she overly strict. She was concerned with the proper operation of the palace, which was her home, rather than her husband's activities. But the poor woman could not escape her husband's wrath, which was actually meant for the governor, whose administrative policies had inspired many hostilities among New Mexico's citizenry.

On April 10, 1663, Don Bernardo López de Mendizabal and his wife arrived at the prison of the Holy Office of the Viceroyalty of New Spain in Mexico City to answer formal charges that had been brought against them. They were assigned to separate cells, and the proceedings began a few days later. The governor's case dragged on as the prosecutors and defense attorneys presented their cases. But Don Bernardo's health was steadily declining. On September 16, 1664, the governor died. He was buried in unconsecrated ground in the corral of the secret prison of the Holy Office. By April 1671, it was recommended that the case should be dropped against the deceased and his memory absolved, although if he were alive, he would have been found guilty on several charges. His remains were exhumed and reburied in the chapel of the Church of Santo Domingo in Mexico City.

Doña Teresa's trial was carried on concurrently with that of Don Bernardo's. Her first formal hearing took place on May 2, 1663. The fearless woman went on her own defense. Doña Teresa stated quite frankly that the book she had been reading was an Italian copy of Tasso's *Orlando Furioso*. Since she had been born and raised in Italy, she did not want to forget the language. Doña Teresa often enjoyed reading out loud to herself. "Surely," she reasoned, "there is nothing sinister about receiving pleasure from a good book." Doña Teresa firmly denounced the charges against her. She admitted that she put onion peels on her feet because it was the only remedy available for corns. The couple was unable to comply with all of their religious obligations due to either ill health or inclement weather.

Although Teresa had been accused of a variety of crimes, she defended herself rather vigorously. She cited reasons why the accusations were inspired by personal enmity and malice toward herself and her husband. She also prepared a long document that described life and society in colonial Santa

Fé. Fortunately, the charges against Doña Teresa were suspended since most of the testimony against her was based on stories circulated by ignorant servants whom she said meddled into her affairs and were scolded for doing so. She asked to have a formal written decision as to her guilt or innocence, but the Holy Office denied her plea. Although this apparently had been done in cases involving the reputations of men, it was not considered essential when the case concerned the good name of a woman. But the intrepid Doña was persistent enough to continue fighting for her rights. Her only true guilt appears to have been the fact that she was the wife of Governor López. However, her contribution to New Mexico's history is quite significant in that her document, which describes life and society in colonial Santa Fé, has served as an invaluable tool for historians studying early New Mexico.

Death, Faith and Life

When the Spanish arrived in the New World, they brought their own death beliefs with roots in European history. During the Middle Ages in Europe, most people lived in crowded houses that had perhaps one large room. All of the family activities took place in this room. For one thing, people seldom bathed in those days. They didn't want to remove the protective layer on their skin, which they thought kept them from getting sick. They would rather cover up body odor with heavy perfume. People would eat and sleep in this large family room. After eating, scraps and bones would be tossed off to one corner of the room, where their pet dogs and cats waited to eat. Food scraps and trash piled up. At night, people rolled out blankets to sleep on, and when they were all sound asleep, rats would come out to eat the scraps and sometimes nibble at their toes.

Soon people started getting sick, and an epidemic called the black plague or Black Death—since bodies turned a bluish/black color—swept throughout Europe. Thousands of people began to die in the cities and towns. Families would place the bodies of those who had died the night before outside their doors to be picked up. Men were hired to ride in wagons called *carretas de la muerte* (death carts) to pick up the bodies for burial in common graves. People cried, and they thought God was punishing them for their sins. They didn't know when the Angel of Death would appear to take another victim. On All Soul's Day, which is the day when they remembered all those who had died before them, people had huge memorial celebrations for the dead.

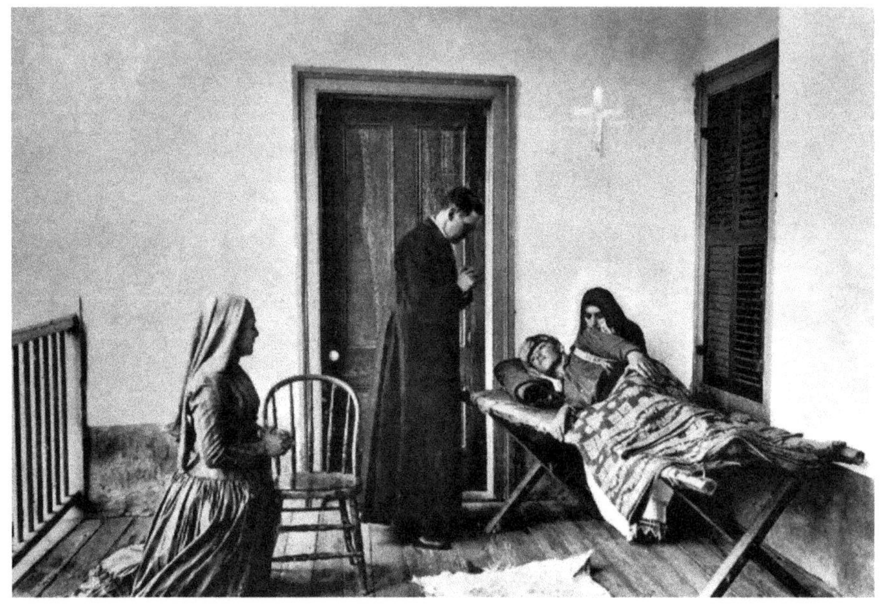

Anointing of the sick. Photographer and date unknown. *Courtesy of the author.*

Most everyone would dress up in costumes that represented skeletons, and they painted or drew dark grotesque creatures. Large black floats with the Death Angel dressed in long flowing black robes and holding a scythe, axe, hatchet or bow and arrow would travel slowly through the streets. Marigolds and other flower petals would be thrown on the ground in front of the float wagons pulled by horses. This custom, or *Danze Macabre*, "Dance of the Dead," spread throughout Europe and became more lavish. People would have kept on dying if it had not been for an accident. Some of the houses caught fire and burned. Thousands of rats scrambled everywhere. It is said that some rivers situated near towns and villages ran black with drowning rats. The Black Death finally started winding down, and people discovered that poor unsanitary conditions had contributed to one of the worst epidemics in history. Life spans were still short, and germs and disease from rodents were still a major problem.

The Spanish Christian rules of dying dating to the macabre horrors and sufferings of the Black Death during this period led to the belief that just before death significant temptations occur, which makes it the most important time to resist temptation and embrace the road to salvation. European Medieval Christian art used gargoyles as a representation of evil to scare people into going to church, and paintings and other mediums depicted earthly temptation and demons luring people into the *infierno* (hell). New Mexico Spanish colonists of the sixteenth century came ingrained with a preoccupation with death and were well aware of consequences faced from not leading a good and honorable life. They knew full well that sudden death could occur while settling an unknown land. This knowledge helped to increase the religious desire for penitence among the settlers, since danger from famine, drought, illness, disease and attacks from hostile Indians and others were facts of life during the first three hundred years of the colony in New Mexico.

Unlike the Danze Macabre of the Middle Ages in Europe, in which the personification of death led a dance of people in order of social precedence to their graves, death rituals in New Mexico took on different forms. The Latin *Memento Mori* (Remember You Will Die) was a predominant theme in the literary efforts of the people, which included religious and non-religious

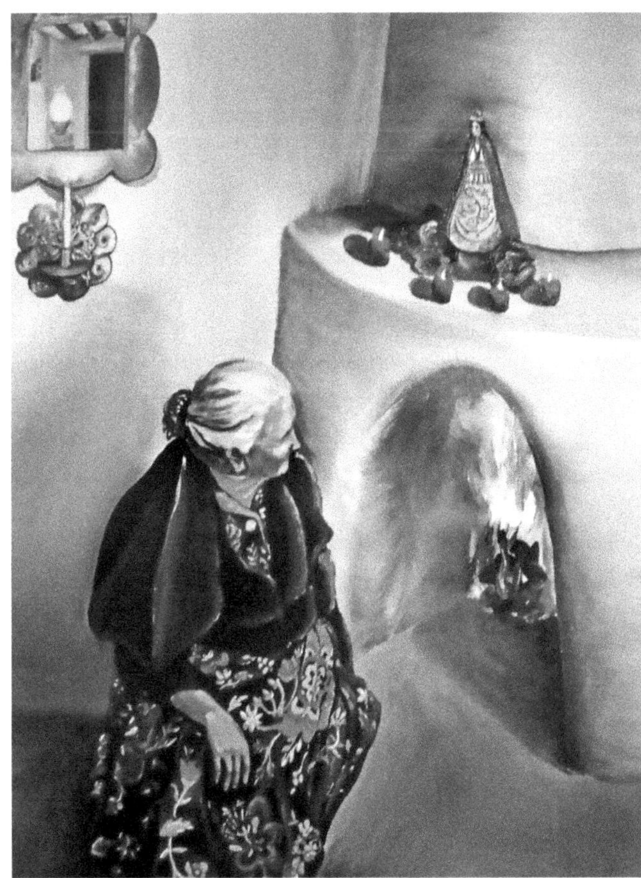

Mañana Viene Mi Hija. Oil on canvas. *©Rosa María Calles, 1987, Kera Anderson collection.*

poetry and musical compositions. The Spanish New Mexicans were also reminded of the punishment they would receive for transgressions through lectures given by community elders and by visual representations of skulls and images of the Angel of Death, known as *la Comadre Doña Sebastiana*, portrayed in New Mexico most often riding in a death cart.

In the isolated mountainous regions of New Mexico, some of the penitential groups used hand-held death images, carved wooden skulls and other associated Angel of Death objects like scythes and sickles in a procession reminiscent of those of ancient origin in Europe. The song "*Acuerdate Mortal* (Remember Mortal)" was sung to impress on the participants the "Ars Moriendi," which was the delineation of what was necessary to experience a good death. This sung poem, or *cántico*, collected in Tomé, New Mexico, around 1855 by Father Juan Bautista Ralliere, "El Padre Eterno," reminds everyone of how fragile their lives are and how the vain glories of earthly life such as avarice, pride, etc., can be a detriment in the final hour. The Spanish guide *Arte de Bién Morir*, which dates back to the fifteenth century and includes certain rules to be followed toward salvation and other aspects and rituals, was used in New Mexico. However, in New Mexico, it was believed that the struggle could continue up to the burial of the deceased. Therefore, relatives and community members had to hold a *Velorio del Difunto* (a wake for the dead)—an all-night vigil with lit candles placed around the body, which rested on a pine wood table. Prayers for the deceased, called *sudarios*, were recited throughout the night, and there was the singing of intermittent songs of farewell, such as "*Adios Acompañamiento* (Goodbye My Family and Friends)." The honored *Doña Sebastiana*, the Venerable Lady (Angel of Death), also reminded them of their inevitable deaths.

New Mexico's Doña Sebastiana is depicted as a large wooden skeleton figure draped in a black shawl with a bow and arrow, riding in a death cart. This image was used in penitential processions. A story is told that once there was a master woodcarver living in Cordoba, New Mexico, who created a large wooden image of death. The figure held a bow and arrow. One day, during a penitential ceremony, the figure released its arrow, and it struck one of the unsuspecting prostrate penitents in the back, and he died. After the customary wake, the dead were carried in a coffin to the cemetery.

Sometimes the cemeteries were located several miles from the homes, farms or ranches of the deceased. The homemade pine coffins were carried on the shoulders of six men at the head of the procession as the family members and villagers sang and prayed along the way. During certain intervals on the path, at areas where wood crosses were affixed to

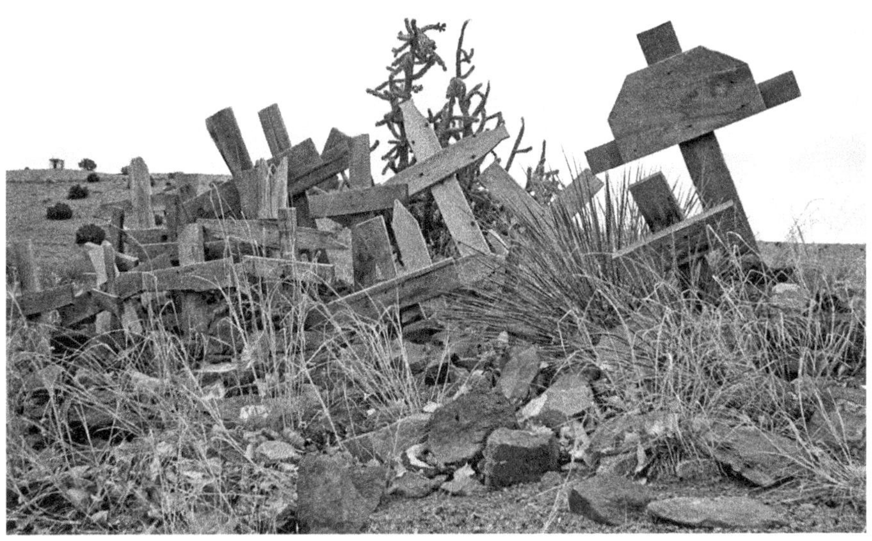

Descanso, near Santa Cruz, circa 1940. Photographer unknown. *Courtesy of the author.*

the ground with piled-up stones, the coffin would be lowered to rest on the ground. During these *descansos*, or rest stops, on the final journey of the deceased, a priest or elder member of the Penitente Brotherhood led prayers. The Penitentes also sang a hymn entitled "*La Encomendación del Alma* (The Commending of the Soul)" and other songs requesting the salvation of the soul and its eternal rest in peace. At the end of the ceremony, a wood cross would be stuck into the ground where other crosses had been placed, and rocks were piled around it. Different members of the family and friends made the crosses, ranging in height from two feet by three feet, for this purpose. The crosses were either simple in design or very elaborate, with grooves, curves or cutout sections. Sometimes village *santeros* were commissioned to make the crosses, or the Penitentes constructed them. The coffin would be raised up again, and the people traveled to the next *descansos* until the Campo Santo (cemetery) was reached. Black had to be worn by everyone in the immediate family of the departed, and no music or dancing was allowed for an entire year after the death.

The Spanish families endured and persevered in New Mexico, in part through ingenuity but mostly because of their tremendous faith. This faith included devotion to reliquaries, the presentation of passion plays and the creation of marvelous wooden religious paintings and sculptures, as well as Christian lyric poetry. These settlers toiled in the fields,

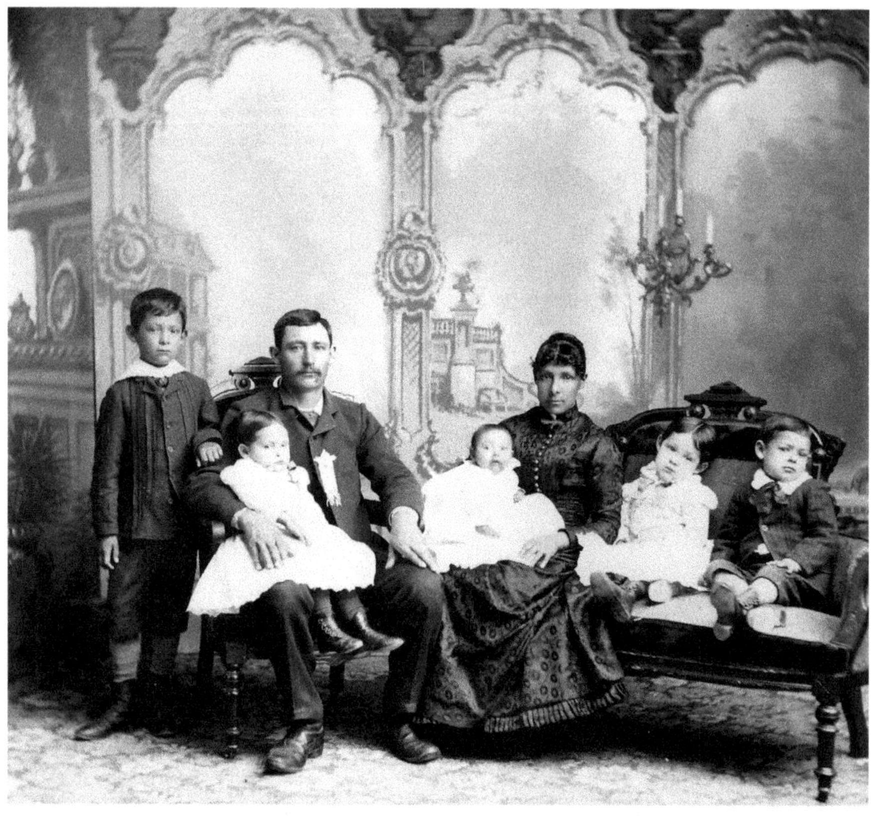

Penitente and family, Las Vegas, New Mexico. James Furlong photo, circa 1879. *Courtesy of the author.*

struggled to survive and often lost their lives just attempting to live from day to day. The Spanish women were major participants as stimulators and preservers of faith and traditions. This was all in conjunction with the Catholic Church in New Mexico, as was common in other areas throughout the colonies.

Spain was gradually transformed during the eighteenth century. By the end of the century, the Old Catholic aristocracy of Spain had ceased to exist. Spain's hold over the colonies grew less and less secure. Mexico won its independence from Spain. The recall of Franciscan missionaries from New Mexico began as early as 1760. New Mexicans took charge of their own spiritual needs. Catholicism in New Mexico not only survived, but it also gained new strength at the close of the nineteenth century and into the twentieth century through the spiritual practices of the Penitentes and Carmelitas.

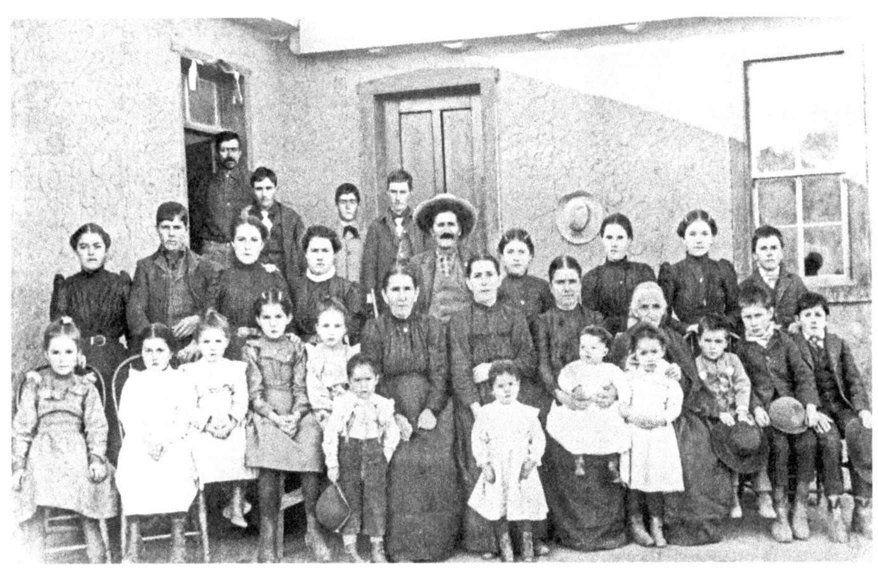

Perfecto Romero family from Los Poblanos, New Mexico, circa 1890. *Courtesy of Harriet Romero.*

The Penitente Brotherhood in New Mexico was very well organized, consisting of the elder members (who often worked at settling disputes within their communities, acting as counselors, being patriotic and law-abiding men), or *Los Hermanos de la Luz* and *Los Hermanos de las Tinieblas* (Brothers of Darkness), sometimes called *Los Hermanos de Sangre* (Brothers of Blood). Los Hermanos de las Tienieblas were occasionally required to perform penitential activities, such as self-flagellation. The officers of each *morada* (chapel) district were selected from Los Hermanos de la Luz and included *El Hermano Mayor*, the Elder Brother, entrusted with the leadership of all members and activities; *El Hermano Celador*, the brother responsible for the safekeeping, care and repair of the *morada*; *El Hermano Enfermero*, the brother responsible for attending to the illnesses and injuries of his fellow members; *El Hermano Mandatorio*, the business manager, who handled all transactions, including transfers of money, food and clothing to those in need; *El Hermano Secretario*, the scribe who recorded and preserved all of the information of value to the membership; and *El Maestro de Novicios*, the teacher of new candidates, who instructed them on the rules and regulations of the brotherhood and orally examined them on the prayers and *alabados*, the knowledge of which was a prerequisite to membership. The remaining brothers performed various duties, such as *El*

Rezador, the leader in reciting the rosary, prayers and *alabados*; *El Pitero*, the flutist, whose shrill, high-pitched notes signaled the start of a procession or religious ceremony or the recitation of a prayer or *alabado* verse; *El Santero*, the maker of holy images of Christ, Mary and the saints; and those brothers who fashioned the *disciplinas*, *matracas*, rosaries with hand-carved wood beads and all of the other paraphernalia essential to the religious ceremonies and activities.

The Carmelitas, sometimes called *Verónicas* and *Terceras*, were the female equivalent of the Penitentes. They were often the wives and relatives of the brothers and like the brothers were dedicated to community service—ministering to the sick, helping the poor and assisting in the burial of the dead. The rituals of the Carmelitas, as those of the *Penitentes*, were just as important to daily and religious life in New Mexico.

By the 1900s, there were approximately 135 active *moradas*, with several thousand members. The chapel area of each *morada* was located in the front room, which contained an altar with *retablos*, hand-carved *santos* and candles. Other items included *bancos* (hand-hewn pine benches), crucifixes, religious pictures in tin frames and wood or tin *nichos*. The inner room served as the penance room and usually contained *la carreta de la muerte* (death cart), *palmilla*

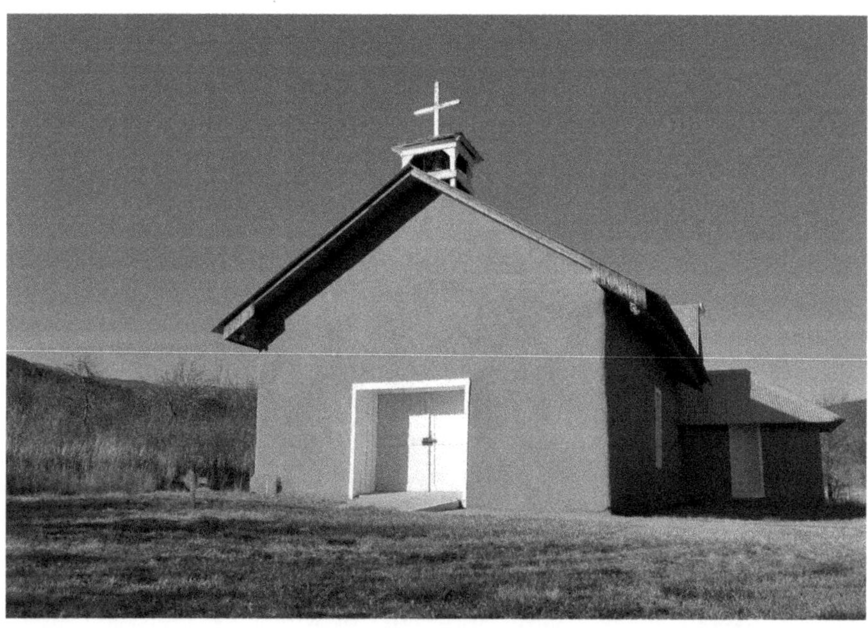

Oratorio de Rociada, New Mexico. *Photograph ©Ramón Juan Carlos de Aragón, 2011.*

disciplinas (fibrous whips), handmade drums, washtubs, washbasins, lanterns, a small wood heater and any other items deemed necessary for religious ceremonies. The interior walls of the morada were whitewashed with *jaspe*, a gypsum powder mixed with water and natural adhesives. On the ceilings usually hung a *manta*, a canvas cloth, pinned down at the corners to catch falling dust and debris. Powdered mica, or *talco*, was added to the adobe stucco of the exterior walls to make them shimmer in daylight or moonlight.

These beautiful moradas, with their confraternities of lay Hispanic religious men and women, which were totally open to anyone for generations seeking physical, emotional and spiritual help, changed in 1846, when New Mexico became a territory of the United States. The newcomers did not understand these centuries-old cultural expressions of faith. *Harper's Weekly* in New York City initially stimulated yellow journalism involving the Penitentes in New Mexico. Sensational stories motivated verbal and written attacks against the brotherhood. Curiosity-seekers searched out Penitente homes and moradas to disturb their Lenten and Holy Week observances and other ceremonies. Many holy images, such as the wooden *santos*, *retablos* and instruments representing the passion sufferings of Christ, were stolen for the private collections of wealthy connoisseurs of art and for museums.

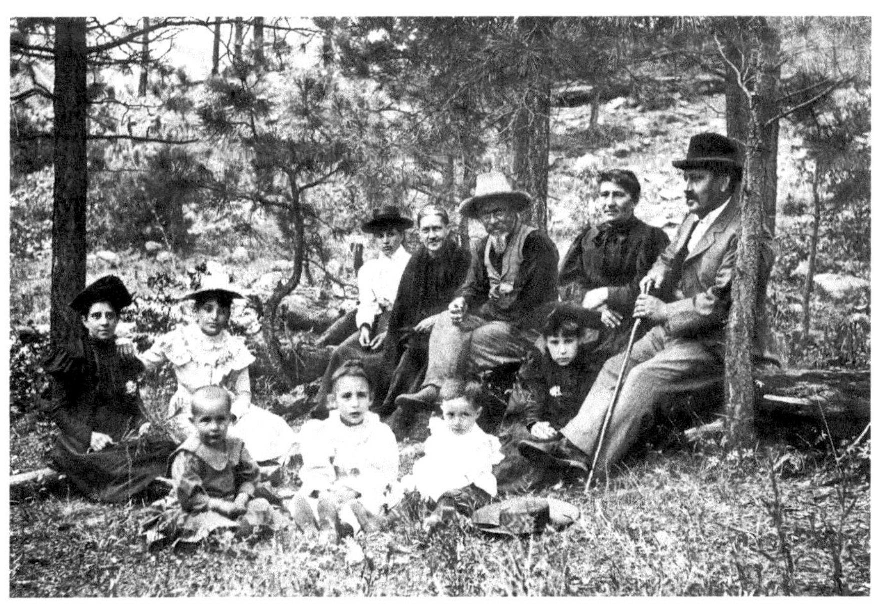

Margarito Romero and family, El Porvenir, owned Romero Mercantile Company, circa late nineteenth century, Las Vegas, New Mexico. Photographer unknown. *Courtesy of the author.*

One thing led to another, and the persecution of the brotherhood in New Mexico culminated with "witch hunts," wherein some of the brothers were pulled out of their homes and assaulted, and their homes and moradas were burned. Some of the Penitentes were jailed for defending themselves. Afraid for their families, the Penitentes and Carmelitas went underground. This religious intolerance against them and the loss of their religious freedoms led to the popular misconception today that they were a secretive cult that practiced ridiculous pagan rituals.

Their faith bound the colony together, but it was also a time when the Spanish grandmothers and mothers provided the backbone and the fortitude to ensure the success of the settlement in New Mexico. They nurtured and maintained the family unit and passed on the only culture they knew—their Spanish heritage—to their offspring. This was a heritage that was forged from the early Iberians through the final independence and birth of Spain in 1492. Synonymous with the creation of the Spanish identity was the use of the term *La Raza Cristiana*, the Christian People. Much of what we know today of these ancient times does not come from the written word but from word of mouth, recording the lives and actions of the people as passed down from one generation to another and eventually written down, each region adapting the stories to its own time and place.

Curanderas

During the Spanish Colonial Period, female Spanish physicians knew how to treat illness and diseases with centuries-old remedies from Spain to try to keep people well and from dying. They also incorporated what they learned from ancient treatments of the indigenous Native American people. Interestingly, the *medicas* (medicine women) used ingredients from plants and other natural elements that would later be used in modern medicines.

When other European and English doctors were treating patients, including kings and queens, with leeches; induced purging, sweating and diarrhea; and prescribing toxic drugs like morphine and opium, Spanish medicine women were ahead of their time in medical treatment and holistic healing.

In today's medical community, research and statistics gathered from patients who are suffering from life-threatening illnesses or addictions reveal that better results in curing, stabilizing or healing an illness to the point of remission are achieved when patients reach into their faith base for emotional or spiritual healing to promote physical healing. In New Mexico

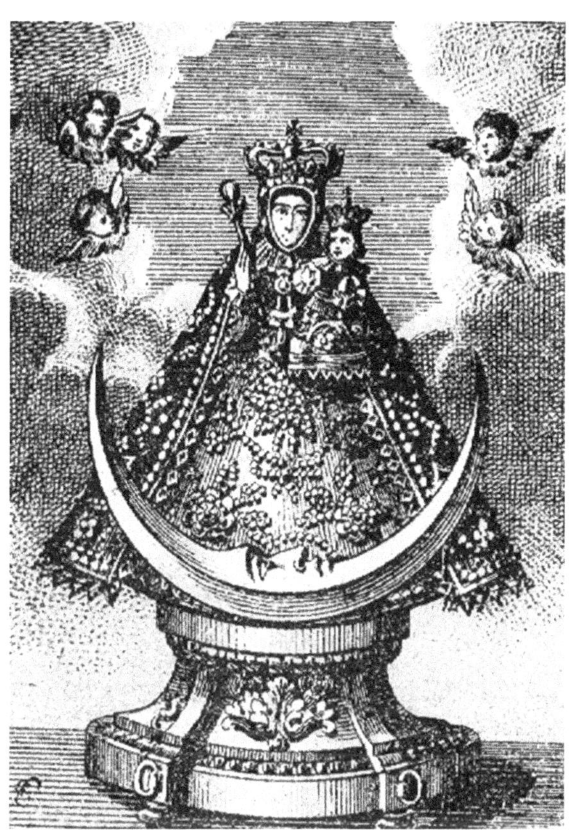

Nuestra Señora de los Remedios. Engraving, 1850. *Author's collection.*

for hundreds of years, it was the Christian faith brought in by the Catholic Church through the Franciscans that was the spiritual influence drawn from to promote healing. After Mexico gained its independence from Spain and the majority of the frays were removed from New Mexico, the faith was kept alive by the people and strengthened through the leadership of the Penitentes and Carmelitas. The lives and spiritual beliefs of the people, including the *curanderas* or *medicas* (medicine women), were centered on their Catholic faith, tradition and culture.

When entering the home of a New Mexico *curandera*, near the entrance was a framed image of the Holy Family, as was found in all New Mexico homes. A shrine called an *altarcito* (little altar) was always located in a special place. A *santo* or *retablo* of *Nuestra Señora de los Remedios* (Our Lady of Remedies) was a central figure, along with the crucifix. Other images of saints who healed were included. San Miguel was the champion archangel who fought evil in all forms. Santa Catalina was prayed to as the protectoress against infection. Santa Lucía protected against diseases of the eyes. Santa Rosalía was prayed to for help against plagues. If someone died, Santa Rosalía was also invoked at the *velorio del defunto* (wake of the deceased) for safe passage of the soul into the afterlife. Santa Veronica helped with healing hemorrhages, and *calaveras* (carved wooden skulls) were present as reminders of death. San Ramón was the patron of childbirth.

Examples of all these saints could be found in a *curandera's* home. The curanderas also had devotional miniatures of Christ, Mary and the saints to carry with them to intercede for healings. The curandera was a servant of God, gifted with knowledge to heal, not through magic, but with a God given skill. Aides used to enhance their prayer lives included *relicarios* (reliquaries), *Agnus Deis* (symbols stamped with the Lamb of God image), *détentes* (images of the sacred heart of Jesus or his mother, Mary) to protect against danger, *escapularios* (scapulars), *rosarios* (rosaries) and various struck medals with other holy images.

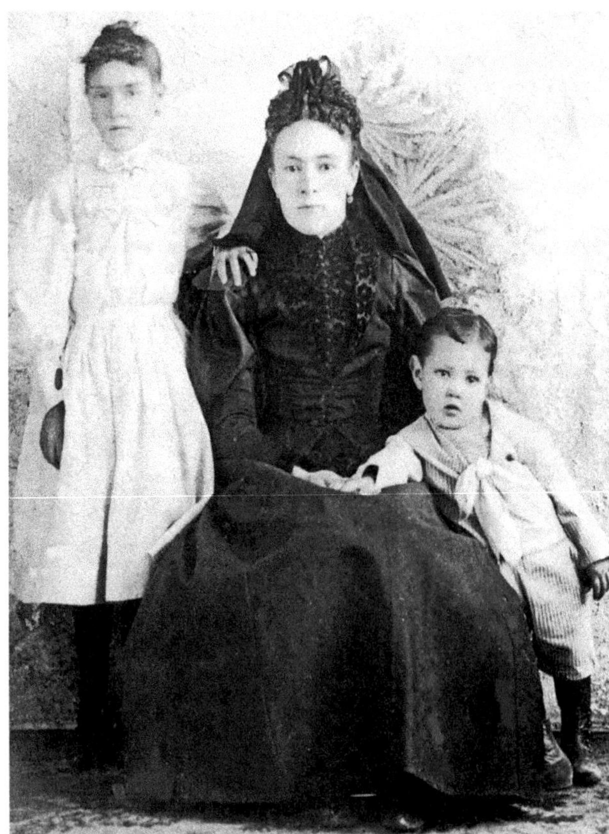

Doña Catalina Mondragón de Valdéz, daughter Virginia Valdéz and Pedro Mondragón. Doña Catalina was a curandera in Mora and Las Vegas, New Mexico. Cabinet photo, circa 1890. *Courtesy of the author.*

In New Mexico in the nineteenth century, Doña Catalina Mondragón de Valdéz was famous as a curandera, and her sister Francisquita was well known as a *partera*, a midwife who delivered many infants. Other women were *sobadoras*, masseuses who not only had the gift of dealing with tense nerves and strained muscles but also knew of or made healthful liniments and lotions that were pleasantly aromatic and soothing for their patients. The dry petals of the Castilian roses, called *Rosas de Castilla*, were another healing plant.

Another *remedio* (remedy) used by New Mexicans was *romero* (rosemary). It was planted next to the doorways for its pretty blue flowers and to keep witches away. The colonists brought *romero* to New Mexico from Spain. According to legend, Mary, the mother of Jesus, draped her blue cloak over a rosemary bush during the Holy Family's Flight to Egypt to escape Herod's soldiers, and this turned the natural color of the plant's blossoms from white to blue. The colonists believed the plant symbolized immortality, and they placed sprigs of it under their pillows to protect them from evil spirits and to keep them from having nightmares.

As a heroic curandera, Doña Catalina learned how to treat various illnesses, injuries and diseases with medicinal herbs in her native Mora Valley as a young girl in the 1870s and 1880s. She is credited with saving countless lives during the influenza epidemic of 1918. New Mexico's state government at the time had very little medical help to offer residents who were victims of the pandemic that ravished the world, killing hundreds of thousands. The curandera placed her own life in danger and spent sleepless days and nights going from town to town and village to village in northern New Mexico and southern Colorado, treating hundreds of patients and then returning to care for those convalescing.

Padre Antonio José Martínez, El Conciliador

Padre Martínez is a well-known figure in New Mexico history. He is recognized as a champion of human rights with powerful political influence, as a religious leader of proportions attached to folk hero status and as a major early force in education, specifically bilingual education. In the area of bilingual education, Padre Martínez was a pioneer and trailblazer who stands out first and foremost as the "Father of Bilingual Education" in the United States with a school he founded in New Mexico in 1833 as an extension of a seminary for the training of native New Mexican priests, which he established during the same year.

Taos, New Mexico, during this period was on the brink of becoming a major center for trade in what was to be the western half of the United States. The Santa Fé Trail brought newcomers into the territory of New Mexico via St. Louis, Missouri, and native New Mexicans traversed the trail eastward. Padre Martínez, as a genius with vision and foresight, saw the direction in which New Mexico and the United States were headed. He knew that education was the key to success for the population of New Mexico, so he founded a school at his own expense.

Before the mid-nineteenth century, Padre Martínez's school had grown considerably in its sphere of influence. It had become a coeducational school—the first in the West. He purchased a printing press, and his students learned to operate it; they helped him print educational materials such as spelling books, readers and math books. This very famous priest also published a newspaper titled *El Crespúsculo* (the *Dawn*), which is recognized as "the first newspaper published west of the Mississippi." Many of his students went on to become newspapermen and publishers themselves and founded newspapers and publishing houses in other villages and cities of New Mexico from the mid- to the late nineteenth century. Due to the very powerful influence of Padre Martinez, many of his students became poets, *santero* artists and craftsmen and performing musicians at this time.

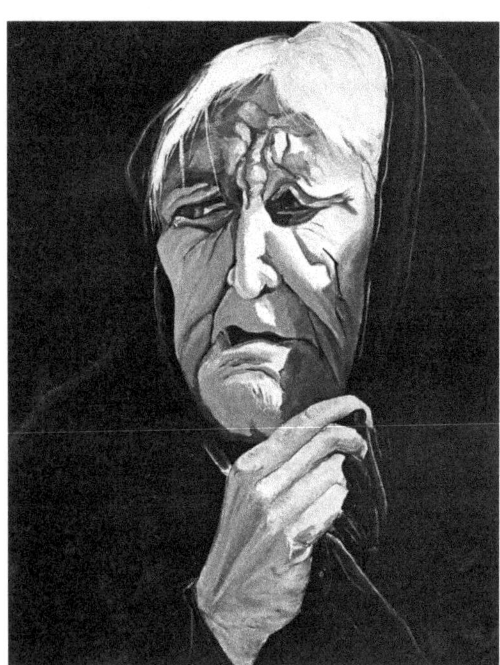

En Luto. Oil on canvas. ©*Rosa María Calles, Father Vincent Chávez Collection.*

Realizing that learning English would be important for New Mexicans due to the steady influx of Americans into the territory, Padre Martínez introduced English into his curriculum, thereby making his school the first truly bilingual school in Spanish and English in New Mexico and the United States. Some of his students even went on to distinguished careers in law, politics, government and education, and several became statesmen, territorial congressmen and territorial senators. Martínez's influence spanned many generations of New Mexicans, and as a larger-than-life Hispanic hero in this country, he defined bilingual education for the future. When Padre Martínez died in 1867, hundreds of people rode on horseback and in wagons or walked on foot for miles from throughout New Mexico to attend his wake and funeral to pay homage to this man whom the territorial legislature called the "honor of his country." This was quite remarkable for his time and place. Also quite remarkable for his era is that he was honored by the Mexican National Congress and the president of Mexico during his lifetime. Newspapers throughout the Republic of Mexico carried his story, and the lasting memories of his remarkable achievements have carried his name into the twenty-first century.

The Republic of Santa Fé

After a revolutionary movement that swept across Mexico with the *Grito de Guadalupe Hidalgo, ¡Que Viva México!*, also called *El Grito de la Independencia* (Cry of Independence), Mexico gained its independence from Spain in 1821. The Mexican government adopted a new constitution in 1834. But the new republic found itself with a series of insurrections as different groups struggled to gain control. Chaos always comes before the calm, but as a result, Mexico was plagued with a continuous unstable government that lasted into the twentieth century.

The national territory of the new republic was vast and sparsely populated in some areas. It was divided into departments, and a governor was appointed to each. Revolutionary movements against the Departmental Plan sprung up in Zacatecas, Sonora, Sinaloa, Tamaulipas, Yucatan, Coahuila and in the provincial areas of New Mexico, which included California, Texas, Arizona and Colorado. Texas gained its independence and established a republic. With the loss of Texas in 1834, the New Republic of Mexico decided to get tough with its remaining territories. The Mexican governor, Albino Perez, arrived in Santa Fé ready to enforce the new laws and rules, including taxation on New Mexico citizens. The new government demanded:

> *Any vehicle carrying goods for sale was levied a two-peso fee before being permitted to enter the capital city of Santa Fé; any individual driving livestock through the streets of the city was assessed a 20 to 25 centavo fee per animal before being allowed to sell them; since Santa Fé was the*

> *only commercial center in the Territory of Santa Fé the ranchers either paid the fees or were forced to drive their cattle or sheep to Chihuahua, Mexico; Santa Fé's influential citizens began to complain to Governor Perez to rescind the tax law, but he, realizing that vaqueros were not available to drive the livestock to Chihuahua, ignored their pleas; also, under the same law, Santa Feans were required to pay a two-peso fee for the privilege of sponsoring theatrical entertainments and fifty centavos for fandangos (dances); All Santa Fé Territory citizens as well as foreigners were ordered to report themselves to the alcalde within three days after their arrival at the capital city of Santa Fé; each person had to state his business and his occupation; anyone failing to do so was subject to a ten-peso fine for each violation of the law as well as a jail sentence.*

Governor Albino Perez began the procedure of deeding over large grants of land to wealthy Mexican and American citizens without considering that many of the poor would become homeless. The priest of Taos, Padre Antonio José Martínez, challenged the governor's actions by writing, "This practice is based on injustice, observed by a government whose tendencies are not in keeping with the advancement of the people."

The taxation of his people began to preoccupy Padre Martínez. The threat of more taxes brought about the publication of his newspaper, *El Crespúsculo de la Libertad* (*The Dawn of Liberty*). He attacked the taxation laws by saying they served no more purpose than to persecute a people who was already tormented by drought and ceaseless Indian raids. Martínez, by defending his people, believed the laws would be revoked through diplomacy, as was done previously when the Mexican Congress changed the tithing system of the church from mandatory to voluntary through the energetic efforts of the priest and his people. But a majority of the Santa Fé citizenry was more inclined to rebel and overthrow the Mexican government at their capital city of Santa Fé. They began to unite, and they formed a large army at Chimayo to attack the capital city. The rebels won over the support of the Pueblo Indians, and they began to organize groups of military forces throughout Santa Fé Territory, including presidio soldiers and officers. Governor Perez, meanwhile, learned what was taking place through spies, but he was confident enough in believing that the native insurgents lacked popular support. After a minor military encounter between Perez forces and insurrectionists, Padre Martínez pleaded for an end to hostilities in his sermons at Our Lady of Guadalupe Church in Taos but to no avail. The rebels were determined. A full-scale rebellion erupted with: "Down with oppression, down with bad government!"

Animosity became more apparent and grew into an outburst of bloodshed in 1837. With a full-scale revolt, Governor Albino Perez received information that a group of rebels was gathering at the Cantón (military encampment) of Santa Cruz de la Cañada near Chimayo, New Mexico. Again feeling confident, Perez launched a surprise attack with a little over two hundred troops. Not realizing that the enemy forces numbered over two thousand, Perez's troops were easily defeated. The governor, along with several other officials who were watching the battle from a distance, quickly escaped. Arriving in Santa Fé, they gathered their possessions and fled south on their way back to Mexico. The revolutionary generals, learning of their escape, sent advance notice to Isleta south of Albuquerque to await their arrival, capture them and have them executed. The Isleta Indians quickly complied with their orders by taking Perez and his men prisoners and cutting off their heads.

After the Battle of Santa Cruz, the revolutionary army marched on the capital and took possession of Santa Fé. They paid homage to La Conquistadora in gratitude for the victory. A provisional government was established, and Don José Gonzales, one of the organizers of the revolt, was placed at the head as provisional governor and commanding general of all the military forces in the Santa Fé Territory. Don José María Ronquillo was selected as the inspector general, and Don Donaciano Vigíl was given the duty of secretary general. Vicente Sánchez Vergara assumed the position of treasurer, and Francisco Baca y Terrus was given the title of *subcomisario* to complete the new administration of the Santa Fé Territory.

Governor Gonzáles's first action after taking office was to call a general meeting, on August 27, 1837, of all the influential citizens throughout the Santa Fé Territory for the purpose of securing their support. But already, discontent permeated the air with Manuel Armijo, a native son who had previously served as governor at Santa Fé.

Political leaders in the southern and northern territory of Santa Fé who still maintained patriotic sentiments toward Mexico and were upset with the arrogance of the rebels in Santa Fé met in council on September 8, 1837, to plan an overthrow of Gonzáles's newly formed regime. The group, meeting in Tomé, developed what they called the Plan of Tomé. They referred to themselves as "citizens who love their country and favor the constitution and the laws, and who fear the anarchy and abuse of property threatened by the Cantón de La Cañada [the name used for the Santa Cruz presidio force in power at Santa Fé designating it as a military presidio camp]." The Plan of Tomé included the following points:

The sole recognized authority would be the prefect of Albuquerque, Antonio Sandoval.

No one would be deprived of his property or rights.

An armed force would be raised, with Manuel Armijo as commander, Mariano Chávez as second in command and Vicente Sánchez Vergara as secretary.

If another commander should later be named, he would continue the same actions as had already been taken.

The Pueblo Indians would not be involved or take sides until the Supreme Government named a government and would in the meantime govern themselves.

Three Isleta natives who had been taught these articles would inform the pueblos of this.

The authority of the Cantón was disavowed.

The commander of the liberating forces would raise money for his army and religiously reimburse owners for anything commandeered.

An extraordinario violento would be sent to inform authorities in Chihuahua and Mexico.

Any contribution made by natives to the commissioners named in Santa Fé would be religiously repaid.

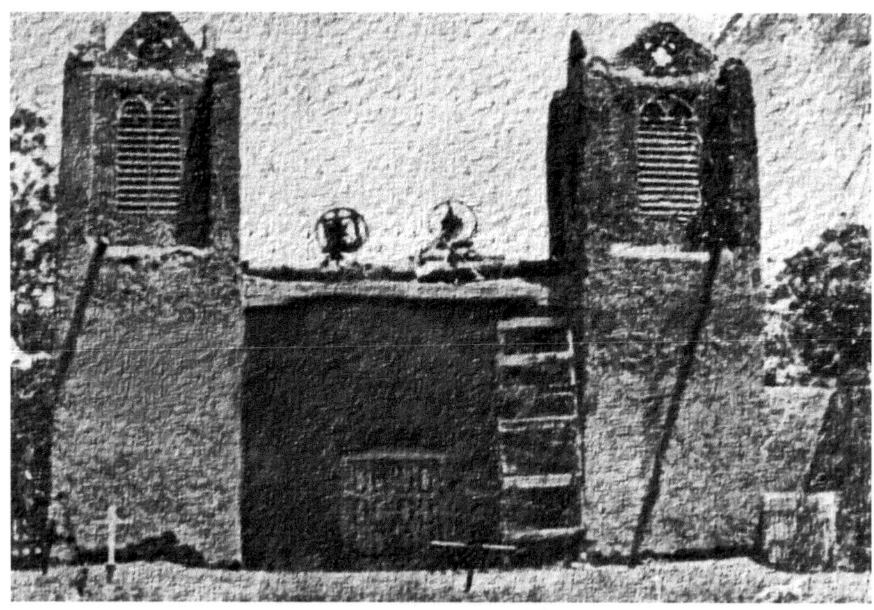

Tomé Church, New Mexico. Nineteenth century, photographer unknown. *Courtesy of the author.*

An army was organized at Tomé with Manuel Armijo as the commanding general for the purpose of taking control of the government at Santa Fé away from Gonzáles and his forces. After asking the Indians to remain neutral, Armijo lost no time and quickly set out with a force of nearly one thousand men toward the capital of Santa Fé. Gonzáles, hearing that a large army was close to his doors, quickly fled the capital to reorganize his forces since most of the able-bodied men of the territory of Santa Fé had returned to their ranches and farms. Taking advantage of a surprise attack, Armijo rapidly marched through Santa Fé and encountered Gonzáles's forces in two battles, where he thoroughly routed the bewildered rebel armies.

Returning to the city of Santa Fé, Governor Armijo went about the business of stabilizing the government of the Territorio de Santa Fé with the approval of the Supreme Government in Mexico City. Armijo was diligently trying to mediate a settlement of the problems affecting the territory, but other revolts were stirring up. Finally, things came to a head again, and Governor Armijo felt compelled to issue an iron-fisted

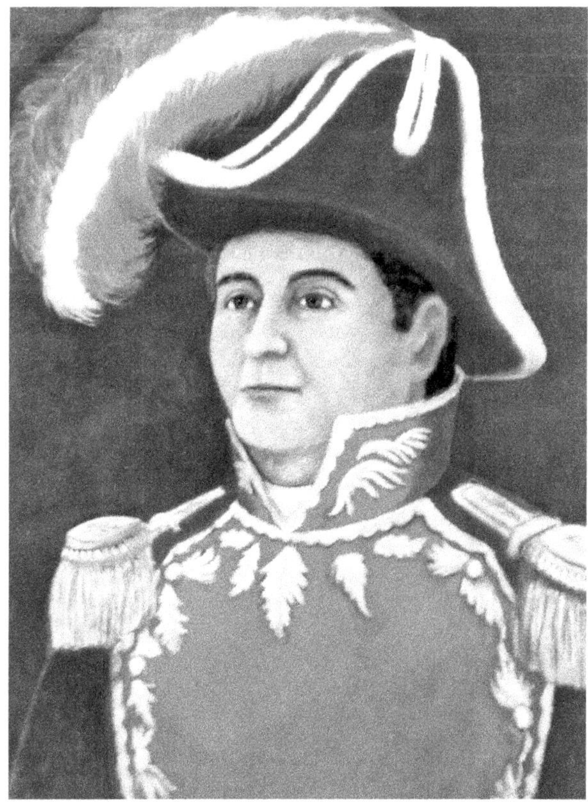

Governor and General Don Manuel Armijo. Oil on canvas, Maximiliano Salazar. *Courtesy of the author.*

proclamation of retribution to those conspiring to develop military movements against the government:

> *The citizen, Manuel Armijo, constitutional governor and principal commandant of arms of the department of Santa Fé:*
>
> *I have just received official news from the municipal council of the villa of La Cañada that the revolutionary, Antonio Vigil, has formed another revolution in the district of Truchas, and that he has already stirred up a number of people. These unhappy ones, worthy of compassion, will be promptly reduced to order by national troops, but as a government interested in the public prosperity, I have to watch that the evils do not increase, and see to it that the wicked do not deceive the people, making them commit crimes and leading them to their ruin. I want the Indians of the country to know that my aim is none other than to sustain the law, punishing only the truly culpable, protecting the ignorant even when they have cooperated with previous revolutions, having been motivated by the seductions and deceits of the promoters. I want them to suffer no hostile treatment however light, nor especially do I want their poor families to suffer the terrible scourge of war to which they are provoked by the rebels of La Truchas at those reunions, as criminal as they are insignificant, so that they forget the clemency and commiseration they have enjoyed until now; but once they are freed from their obstinacy and backsliding, one must work in another manner, and therefore I am convinced that the blame always falls on the poor ignorant Indian who knows not what he does. I am warning them, so that they may not be deceived, so that they may close their ears to the invitations, and so that they may live in peace in the confidence that the government values them, but if in spite of this they take part in the revolution, they may not afterwards complain nor plead ignorance, for then the rigor of the law will fall equally on everyone. Santa Fé, January 19, 1838*

By January 27, 1838, Governor and General Armijo had received additional support from Mexico with the arrival of a military force of Veracruz dragoons under the command of Lieutenant Colonel Justiniani. After learning that a force of 1,300 rebels was gathering about seventeen miles north of Santa Fé, Armijo and Justiniani marched out to meet them. Governor Armijo was not inclined to launch an attack, but Captain Muñoz of the Veracruz dragoons asked for permission to lead a charge. After receiving Armijo's approval, Muñoz followed through with an unmerciful onslaught, scattering the rebel forces and striking down all vestiges of resistance.

Governor and Commanding General Manuel Armijo returned to Santa Fé in triumph. Armijo, being a native New Mexico son, was more inclined to relieve tensions in favor of New Mexico. The Santa Fé Territory prospered economically, but resentment fostered by the revolt proved to be Armijo's undoing with the entry of American forces in 1846.

A Concealed History

Many mysteries abound in New Mexico that are known throughout the world. People are still intrigued by the question of how Billy the Kid died. Researchers still wonder what led up to the demise of the Kid on that dark night of July 14, 1881. Some scholars believe Billy was set up by Sherriff Pat F. Garrett in a conspiracy that involved Pete Maxwell. Pete owned the ranch in Fort Sumner in whose bedroom Billy the Kid died. The belief is that Maxwell conspired with Garrett to keep his sister, Paulita, who was pregnant with the Kid's child, from running away with him. Others still think that Garrett accidently stumbled onto the Kid while talking with Maxwell on his bed. Billy backed up into the bedroom unexpectedly, asking, "*¿Quién es?* (Who is it?)" This was apparently in reference to Garrett's deputies, who were posted outside, and Billy didn't recognize them. Once he stepped inside, Garrett shot him.

Another famous puzzle in New Mexico is the well-known mysterious disappearance of Albert Jennings Fountain and his eight-year-old son, Henry, on February 1, 1896. Both of them vanished into thin air near the White Sands as they traveled home to Mesilla in their buckboard. Their bodies were never found, but blood near the wagon indicated a crime. No one was convicted, and now, over one hundred years later, this unsolved murder is still being investigated and is the subject of many books and documentary films.

For some, solving mysteries is a full-time job. In the world of unexplained ancient maps, for example, people are still stunned by the enigma of the Piri Reis map. This amazing map dating to 1513, drawn on gazelle skin and discovered in 1929, contains details of the Arctic region about three hundred years before it was discovered. The map was drawn by Piri Reis, an Ottoman-Turkish admiral and cartographer. Reis claimed he developed and drew his mind-boggling map from other ancient maps he had studied. His puzzling map shows the Arctic coastline, as it would have appeared ice-free around 4000 BC. Another similar enigma is the Oronteus Finaeus map

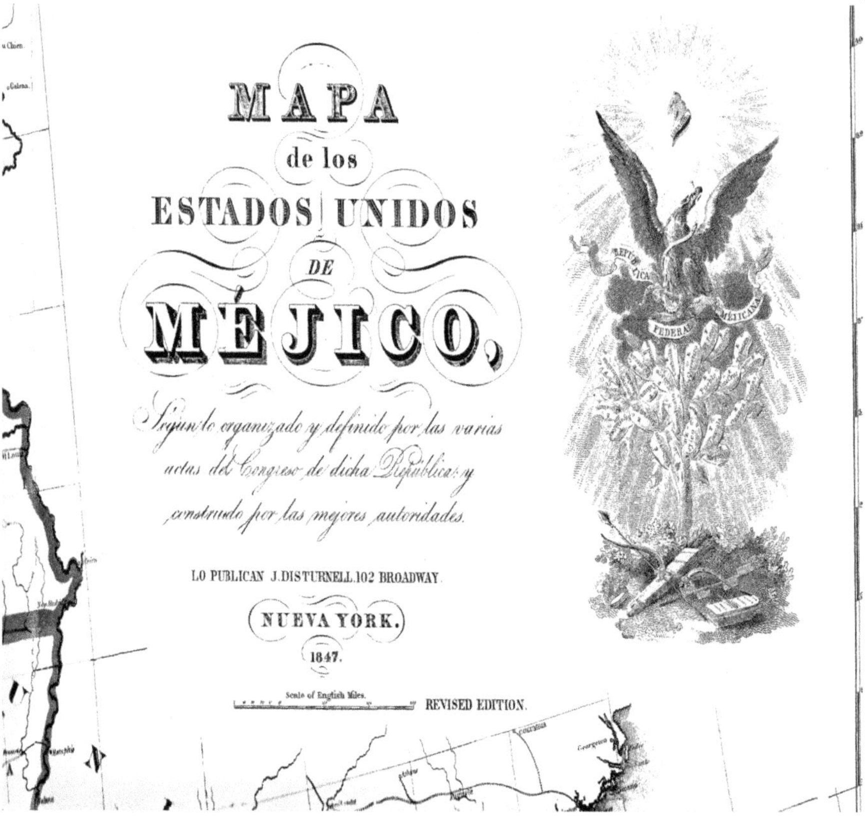

MAPA
de los
ESTADOS UNIDOS
DE
MÉJICO,

Según lo organizado y definido por las varias actas del Congreso de dicha República y construido por las mejores autoridades.

LO PUBLICAN J. DISTURNELL, 102 BROADWAY.

NUEVA YORK.

1847.

Scale of English Miles. REVISED EDITION.

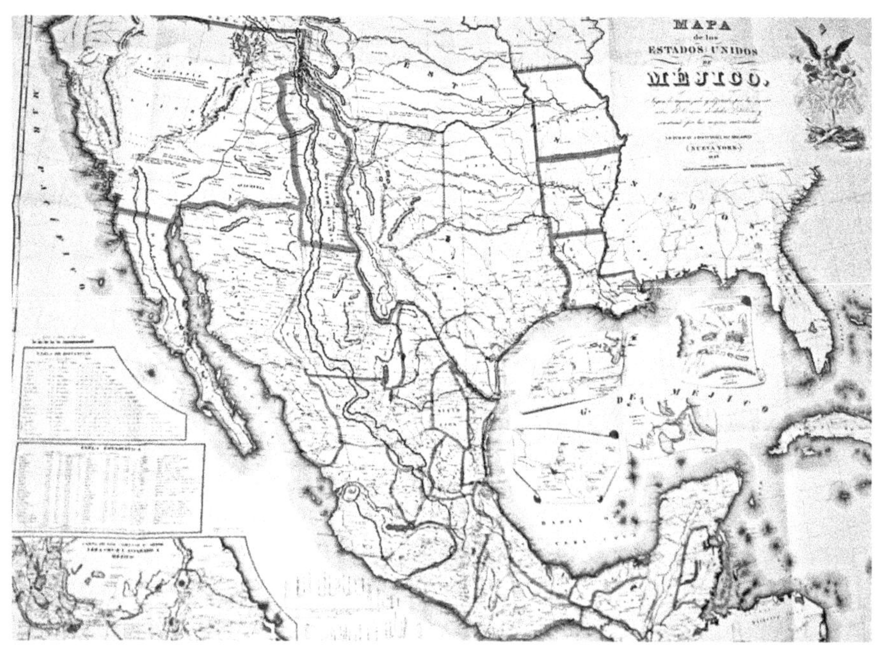

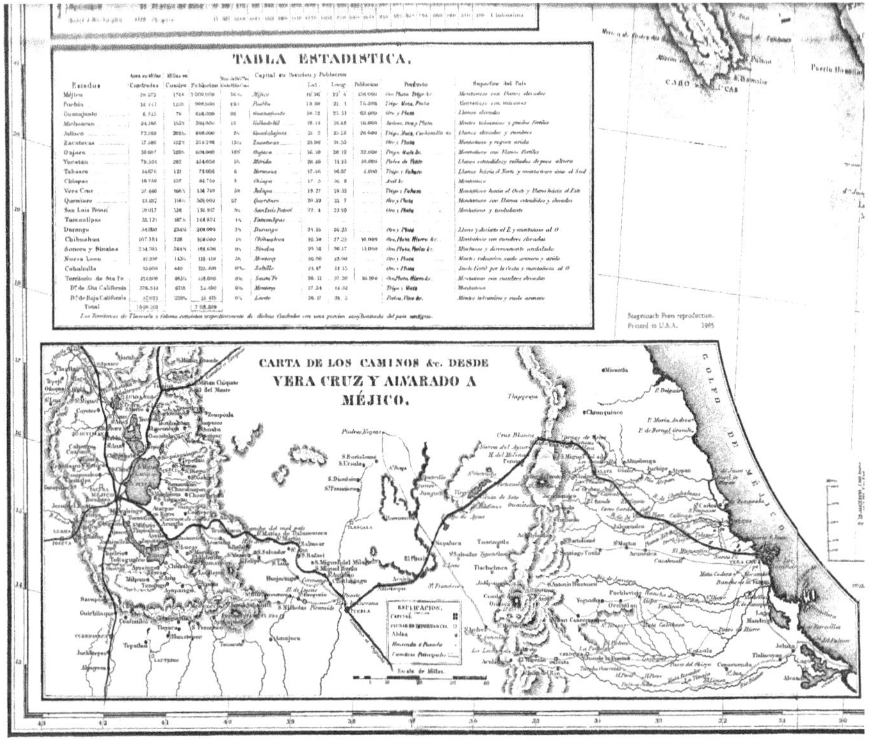

Above: *Tabla Estadística* (Table of Statistics), detail showing the capital, position and population of Santa Fé Territory. From the Disturnell Map. *Courtesy of the author.*

Opposite: Detail from the Disturnell Map, part of the Guadalupe Hidalgo Treaty on Southwestern Boundaries, 1848, reproduced from 1846 to 1850 and then, in 1858, showing the territory of Santa Fé. Jack D. Rittenhouse, Stagecoach Press, Santa Fe, 1965. *Courtesy of the author.*

drawn in 1531. The famous cartographer Finaeus shows Antarctica ice-free, with flowing rivers, drainage patterns and a clear coastline. Some of the mountain ranges shown were only recently discovered. Oronteus Finaeus was one of the most accurate mapmakers of the Old World. Other strange maps include seven fragile map books from 4,200 years ago from China that seem to indicate that Chinese sailors and explorers discovered America at that time. The *Catalán Atlas* from the Mallorcan cartographic school in Spain, produced around 1375, is also an enigma. This atlas was one of King Charles V's most prized possessions. New Mexico has its own cartographic mystery. A very unusual map, called the Disturnell Map, was produced by John Disturnell in 1846 and includes the boundaries of Santa Fé Territory!

John Disturnell claimed to have used ancient Spanish maps of the viceroyalty of New Spain to develop and design his map of the Republic of Mexico, which includes the Santa Fé Territory. Disturnell's map, published in New York, was officially adopted by the Mexican National Congress and the United States Congress. In Spanish, it reads, "*Mapa de los Estados Unidos de Méjico…Según lo organizado y definido por las varias actas del Congreso de dicha República y construido por las mejores autoridades.*" (The United States of Mexico Map…as organized and defined by the various acts of the congress of said republic and constructed by the best authorities). The map shows the boundaries of the Mexican Republic's nineteen states at the time and the borders of the territories of upper and lower California, Texas, New Mexico and the territory of Santa Fé. Disturnell's map shows Santa Fé Territory as bounded to the west by the Río Grande or Río Bravo del Norte from its mouth all the way to the Gulf of Mexico. The Río Grande is the fifth-largest river in North America, with a length of 1,900 miles. Along the border across from the Río Grande are the areas of Nuevo México, Chihuahua, Coahuila, Nuevo León and Tamaulipas. The eastern border of the Santa Fé Territory is the Nueces River and Indian Territory, and the northern border is the Arkansas River. The San Juan Mountains of southwestern Colorado were a part of the territory of Santa Fé. Texas lies opposite of the Nueces River. The Sierra Nevada Mountains, which are now in Nevada, lie in this territory, as do Corpus Christi, Padre Island and part of Corpus Christi Bay. This means that Santa Fé Territory at one time had a coastline! The capital city of Santa Fé Territory is listed as Santa Fé. The population of the territory is 150,000, and the capital city is listed with 10,100 residents. The entire area of the territory of Santa Fé comprises 214,800 square miles.

The history of the territory of Santa Fé has lain hidden now for over one hundred years—or has it? On February 2, 1848, the governments of the United States and Mexico signed the Treaty of Guadalupe Hidalgo, which officially ended the Mexican-American War. The treaty set the southern and western limits of New Mexico, as established by James Disturnell. All required signatures and seals of the governments of Mexico and the United States of America legally validated the document in perpetuity. Difficulties as to boundaries arose from the beginning. American surveyors, ironically, were legally bound by the Disturnell Map, as approved by both congresses. Different interpretations caused by the map might have led to confusion about the boundaries of Santa Fé Territory and the actual boundaries of New Mexico. President James K. Polk appointed Nicholas Philip Trist as peace commissioner in early 1847 to negotiate a peace treaty. John Disturnell's map was to be used to set boundaries.

New Mexico on Disturnell's map was shown much narrower than what it is today and ran much farther north than the present-day state of New Mexico. The Río Grande was set as the eastern boundary, and the southern line was near El Paso del Norte, present-day El Paso, Texas. New Mexico extended north to present northwestern Colorado. The Republic of Texas was bounded by the Gulf of Mexico, where it is joined by present-day Oklahoma and Louisiana. The Texas Panhandle on the map stretched from the Arkansas River, and the western flank was bounded by the territory of Santa Fé. President Polk was having political battles with the Whig Party, so he approved a treaty with Mexico with boundaries as set by James Disturnell's map. The U.S. Congress and Senate approved the boundaries as set by the treaty on March 16, 1848. The treaty was ratified by the Mexican Republic on May 30, 1848. The boundaries of New Mexico were always contested by the Republic of Texas.

On October 2, 1835, Texas officially revolted against Mexico. Previously, both Santa Fé Territory and the Texas Territory had entertained thoughts of being admitted as states to the United States of Mexico. However, after independence in 1821, Mexico went through a series of revolutions and numerous installations of new governments under new presidents and congresses, so no action was undertaken on admitting other states into the union. Immediately after Texas gained independence in 1836, the newly formed government sought to expand its boundaries. The Nueces River had been the established southern boundary of the Texas Territory under Mexican and Spanish rule. Now, the Republic of Texas, in a congressional act dated December 19, 1836, claimed the borders of the Santa Fé Territory as part of the borders of Texas and incorporated this area on maps of the newly formed republic.

The first step taken to exercise control of Santa Fé Territory took place on June 19, 1841, when a Texas military force, under the pretext of establishing trade, entered the area. The treasury of the new republic was depleted and near bankruptcy. It was determined that gaining control of the Santa Fé Trail and redirecting trade from Missouri and the capital city of Santa Fé would provide the country with desperately needed commerce and goods. Also, the money that the republic was printing was worthless. A Texan military force headed by General Hugh McLeod, a West Point graduate, was composed of five companies of infantry and one of artillery. The force set out from Kenney's Fort on Bushy Creek, twenty-five miles north of Austin,

Texas. The Texan army was captured by a superior Santa Fé army after crossing into the Llano Estacado (Staked Plaines) at Laguna Colorada, near present-day Tucumcari, on October 5, 1840. The Texan army surrendered without firing a shot. Other minor attempts of controlling the Santa Fé Trail included an attack on the town of Mora by Colonel Warfield and his force. Other Texan troops committing depredations were under the command of Captain John McDaniel. In May 1843, Colonel Snively, with some Missouri volunteers, commanded an army that was organized in northern Texas. They attacked traders on the Santa Fé Trail, and a battle ensued near the Arkansas River, where twenty-three Santa Fé troops were killed and one hundred were injured.

President Sam Houston authorized the Snively Expedition on February 16, 1843. General Jacob Snively entered New Mexico in June 1843 and was joined by remnant forces of Charles A. Warfield that had been defeated by

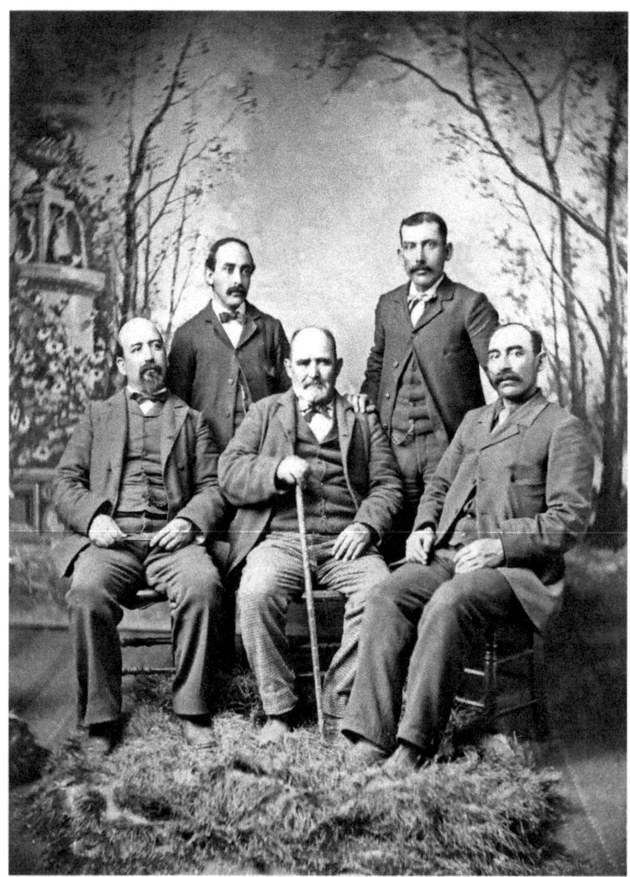

Las Vegas merchants: Patricio, Porfirio, Manuel, Cruz and Anselmo Gonzales. James Furlong photo, date unknown. *Courtesy of the author.*

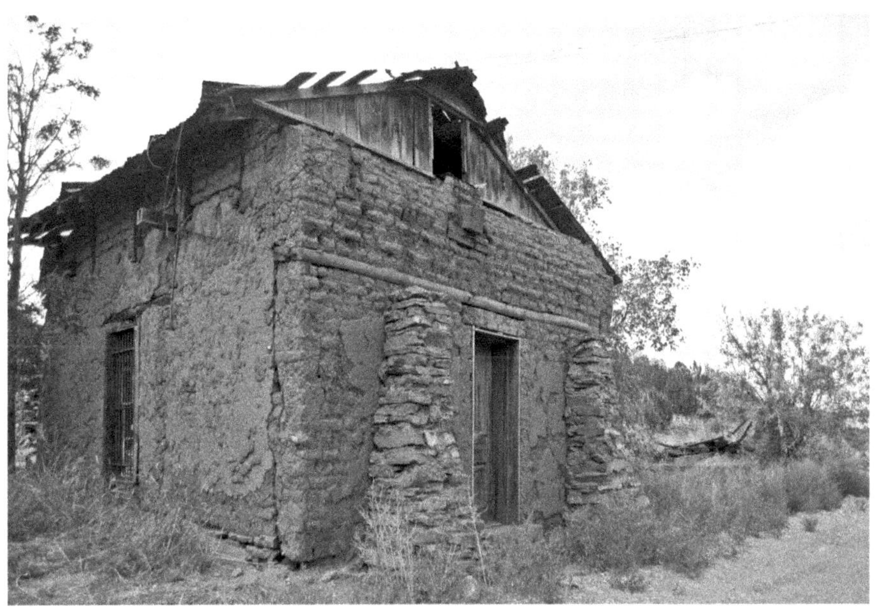

La Tiendita, ruins of a San Miguel village grocery store. *Photograph ©Ramón Juan Carlos de Aragón, 2011.*

Santa Fé Presidio soldiers. Antonio José Chávez, an early Santa Fé Trail merchant en route from Santa Fé to St. Louis, Missouri, and his party were attacked and murdered by John McDaniel and his Texan army on U.S. territory. Colonel Stephen Watts Kearney sent out a force of U.S. troops to engage the Texans. Some of McDaniel's troops escaped, but other Texan soldiers were captured, imprisoned and hanged.

The Santa Fé Trail, which was established in 1821 by Santa Fé Hispanic merchants and U.S. merchants, rapidly became an international road that stimulated massive changes in United States commerce and growth. By 1843, hundreds of wagons traveled back and forth from Santa Fé to Missouri, affecting the economic growth of the United States. Needless to say, both the floundering Republic of Mexico and the bankrupt Republic of Texas set their sights on the trail. Mexico, however, was much too involved in widespread internal problems dealing with Spanish sympathizers and continuous revolts.

Since territorial boundaries between the United States and Mexico were largely ambiguous, Texas president Mirabeau B. Lamar supported a group of Mexican influential citizens and Texans who were attempting to revolt against Mexico and establish the República del Río Grande with the capital city at Austin, which would largely comprise most of the territory of Santa Fé as delineated by the Disturnell Map.

Lamar referenced a United States and Mexico map published by I.T. Hinton and Marshall in 1832, printed in London, England, which showed the Santa Fé Territory as part of what was called "Arkansas Territory, bordered south by the Río Grande, New Mexico, and Mexico and bordered by the United States and Texas." The Texan president was in support of the new Republic of the Río Grande, which had governmental leaders and a flag. He thought it could be annexed into the Republic of Texas, and the lucrative trade of Santa Fé, and the Santa Fé Trail, would then fall into Texan hands.

Problems with the Disturnell Map complicated the situation. El Paso del Norte, for example, was shown in two different locations. Present-day El Paso was shown one hundred miles east of its true location. Parts of New Mexico would then appear either in the United States or in Mexico. The matter of the Disturnell Map was not resolved by the United States and Mexico until 1854, with the Gadsden Purchase. American occupation of some areas was, therefore, protested by Mexico.

United States boundary surveys were not completed until 1856. Disturnell Maps, showing the boundaries of the territory of Santa Fé, were printed

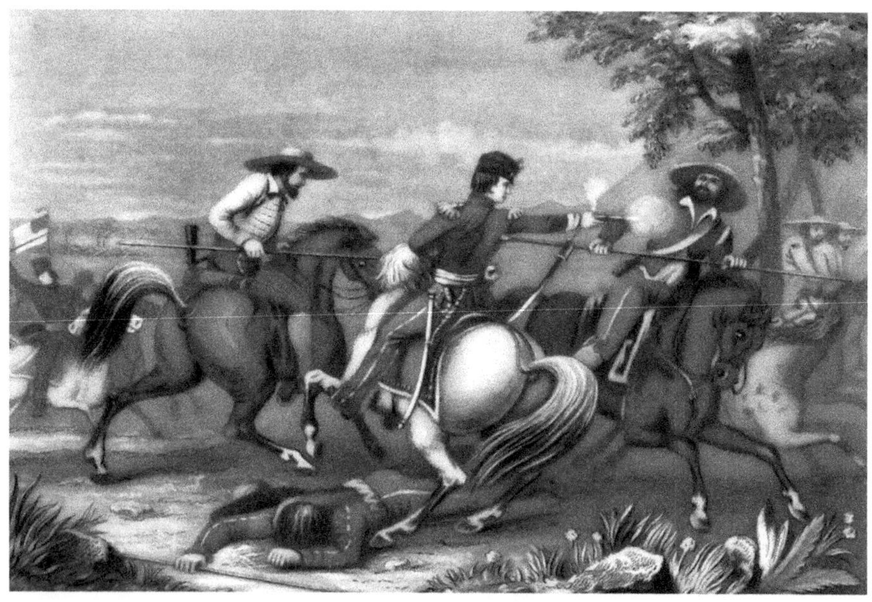

Mexican-American battle scene. Unknown artist and location. *Courtesy of the author.*

from 1846 to 1858. Major changes in boundaries were not given. This might mean that General Stephen Watts Kearney and his expeditionary force of Missouri volunteers, who were not officially sanctioned by President James K. Polk and the United States Congress when they proclaimed the takeover of New Mexico on August 22, 1846, were committing an unlawful act by trying to take over the wrong territory. Territory of Santa Fé citizens would not have known what he was referring to, and Kearney and his forces would have been allowed to travel south past the Río Grande to Nuevo México—New Mexico. He and his forces erroneously thought they were taking over Santa Fé, but in reality, according to the stipulations of the *Tratado de Guadalupe Hidalgo* (Treaty of Guadalupe Hidalgo), his group was committing depredations.

In 1846, New Mexico was invaded by an American military expeditionary force under the command of Brigadier General Stephen Watts Kearney, which was not entirely sanctioned by the U.S. government. The expedition was to test the waters to see if the inhabitants would peaceably swear allegiance to the United States. Contrary to the popular myth promoted by most historians that Kearney executed a peaceful, bloodless conquest of the territory, New Mexican forces fought the American occupation ceaselessly for several years, winning some battles and many skirmishes and engagements. The military commanders of New Mexico officially declared war against the hostile actions of the United States on January 20, 1847. The most famous battle was the Battle of Red River Canyon (La Batalla del Canyon Río Colorado), which took place on May 26, 1847, during which New Mexican forces numbering several hundred, under the command of General Manuel Cortez, thoroughly routed and defeated the American dragoons under Major Edmonson.

The Hispanic New Mexico military forces were supported by large numbers of Apache, Comanche and Kiowa Indians. Pueblo Indians fought with the Hispanos against the Americans in other battles. The trained military of the New Mexican presidios (forts or garrisoned posts) fought furiously in battles at San Juan de los Llanos, El Cerro de Villanueva, Santa Cruz de la Cañada, Brazito, Taos, Las Vegas, Embudo, Mora, the Canadian River, Santa Clara, La Cienega, Anton Chico and Arroyo Hondo. New Mexican forces were victorious at Arroyo Hondo; the first Battle of Mora, where two separate engagements took place; Red River; and the Canadian River, where Comanche, Cheyenne and Apache allies joined Cortez. The Pawnee, Arapahoe and Kiowa joined Hispanos in other battles. About twelve major battles were fought on New Mexico territory, as well as dozens of skirmishes,

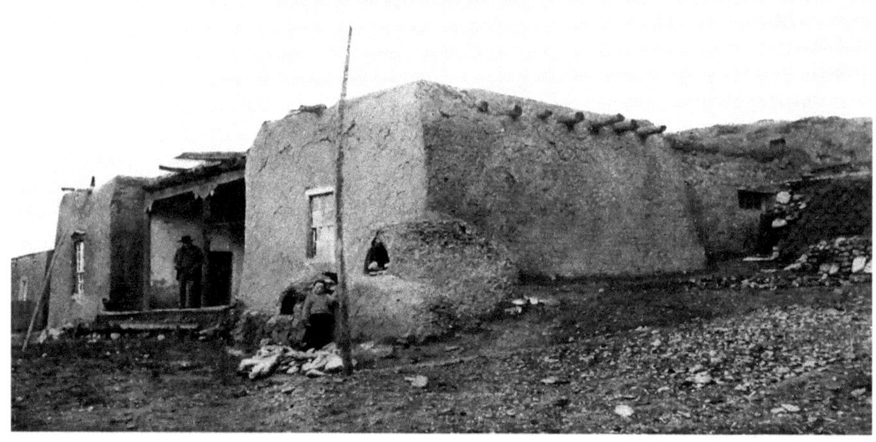

Santa Fé adobe. Southwest Arts & Craft Co. photo postcard. *Courtesy of the author.*

in which hundreds of New Mexican soldiers and many women and children lost their lives in heroic and courageous defense of their homeland.

Military action in New Mexico did not cease until 1851, when New Mexico officially became a territory of the United States. However, the Indian tribes allied with the New Mexicans continued to fight until the turn of the century. Interestingly, the number of American and New Mexican casualties was diminished, and information of the New Mexican victories was suppressed so that this would not inspire or incite more resistance against American forces. The sheep industry in New Mexico suffered as a result of the war, since thousands upon thousands of sheep were slaughtered to break the backs of the inhabitants. A slash-and-burn policy was also enforced by American troops.

After this, the U.S. dragoons' appropriation of livestock, crops, homes and land became commonplace, to the point of creating friction and animosity among the inhabitants. Adding to the friction was the destruction of the churches of San Geronimo de Taos, Santa Gertrudis de Mora, Nuestra Señora de los Dolores de Las Vegas and Santa Clara, as well as the village of Santa Clara near the Wagon Mound on the Santa Fé Trail, by Kearny's troops during battles with Santa Fé forces. Mexican citizens had sought sanctuary in the churches, but the dragoons saw them as fortresses to be destroyed by mortar and cannon fire.

The Treaty of Guadalupe Hidalgo between the United States and Mexico was signed on February 2, 1848, and ratified by the U.S. Senate on March 10, 1848. With the ratification of the treaty, New Mexico, California and

Colorado were annexed to the United States. The treaty brought the war to an end, but New Mexico had felt no real loyalty to Mexico, and Mexico had very little interaction with the government in Santa Fé. New Mexico was a U.S. military department, and Hispanos from New Mexico, in a tremendous display of courage and heroism, desperately tried to protect their homeland from the invaders.

The Bataan Death March

Many New Mexico families tell stories about loved ones who fought in the Philippine Islands during World War II in the 200th and 515th Coastal Artillery Units from New Mexico. The war began for the 200th Coast Artillery with Japanese bombers on December 8, 1941. The more than 78,000 American and Filipino soldiers, in addition to some 20,000 Filipino civilians, were commanded by Major General Edward King. The major general felt he had no choice but to surrender; otherwise, he said, "Bataan would be known as the greatest slaughter in history." The New Mexico Brigade, or the 200th Coast Artillery Regiment, was deployed to the Philippines in September 1941 with 1,800 men; 1,000 died during the march, along with 9,000 Filipino soldiers.

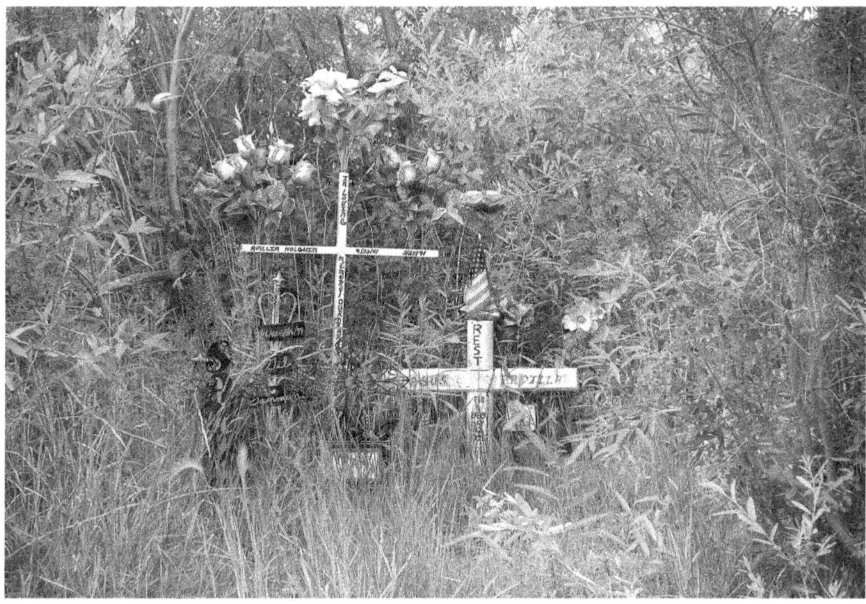

Descanso. *Photograph ©Ramón Juan Carlos de Aragón, 2011.*

Alberto and Salvador were sons of Eloisa Gallegos from Albuquerque, New Mexico. Alberto did not fight in World War II, but Salvador and a close friend he called Vallejos were two of the men taken as prisoners who survived the Bataan Death March. Vallejos was one of the random men chosen on the Death March by the Japanese to torture beyond the disease, starvation, cruelty and horrendous conditions they already endured. He lived, but the memories were so painful that he cried when he talked about the war. Some were tortured by having their nails and teeth pulled out with pliers. He was beaten, stabbed and cut with their bayonets. He often showed the scars across his chest and back to prove that what he was saying was true. Vallejos's cousin Nick Gallegos, also of Albuquerque, said they ate cats, slugs, rats, dried insects, python and monkey. If they were caught eating or drinking water from the infested puddles along the path, they would be tortured, but many were beheaded on the spot. The soldiers agreed that if they were killed, those who survived should cut the flesh from their legs to eat to keep from dying of starvation. They survived the war but remained ill for the rest of their lives. A third of the POWs who survived died within the first year of freedom from complications and illnesses suffered during confinement. Another cousin, Salomon, was reported missing in action, and his body was never recovered. His mother, Rebecca, received word of his death after the war ended, along with his awarded Purple Heart.

The survivors of the Death March were transported to another island aboard Japanese "death ships." Leonardo Vallejos, the son of Francisco Vallejos, and his cousin Rojelio Vallejos, from Tomé, New Mexico, were two of the men transported on one of the death ships, which were mistakenly bombed by American pilots. The Japanese deliberately filled their ships with American prisoners. Rogelio Vallejos was tortured by the Japanese and returned to the United States as an exchange prisoner. He had been there since 1941. Leonardo was on a ship that was sunk, but he survived. Another ship picked up the survivors. Just as the second ship was nearing the island, the ship was also sunk. Leonardo swam ashore but was again captured by the Japanese. Eleven thousand American prisoners died on the death ships, and 11,500 American troops died in confinement. Those who survived the transfer would spend the next forty months in dreadful conditions in confinement camps, with very little food, water or clothing. Jose S. "Chaveta" Chávez, a survivor living in Valencia County, New Mexico, stated:

The Japanese threw me into a mass grave, and dirt was thrown over me and the rest of the dead, decaying soldiers. I don't know how, but I managed to crawl over many dead bodies and saw a light opening at the top of the grave. It took me two hours, but I made it out. The Japanese were totally stunned. My buddies carried me back to the barracks. Two weeks later, they buried me again. It began to rain, and I came back to life.

Bibliography

Ashford, Gerald. *Spanish Texas: Yesterday and Today*. Austin, TX: Jenkins Publishing Co., 1971.

Bancroft, Hubert Howe. *History of Arizona and New Mexico, 1530–1888*. San Francisco: The History Co., 1889. Reprint, Albuquerque, NM: Horn and Wallace, 1962.

Bannon, John Francis. *The Spanish Borderlands Frontier, 1513–1821*. Albuquerque: University of New Mexico Press, 1974.

Bolton, Herbert E. *Coronado, Knight of Pueblos and Plains*. Albuquerque: University of New Mexico Press, 1949.

Boxer, C.R. *The Church Militant and Iberian Expansion, 1440 1700*. Baltimore, MD: Johns Hopkins University Press, 1978.

Boyd, E. *Popular Arts of Spanish New Mexico*. Santa Fé: Museum of New Mexico, 1974.

Bradford, Prince L. *Spanish Mission Churches of New Mexico*. Cedar Rapids, IA: The Torch Press, 1915.

Bruce Bower. "Prehistoric Hand Axes Older Than Once Thought." *Science News*, September 3, 2009.

Burke, James T., Reverend. *This Miserable Kingdom*. Las Vegas, NM: Our Lady of Sorrows Church, 1973.

Cabeza de Baca, Fabiola. *We Fed Them Cactus*. Albuquerque: University of New Mexico Press, 1954.

Cabeza de Baca, Vincent. *La Gente: Hispano History and Life in Colorado*. Historical Society of Colorado, 1998.

Castañeda, Carlos E. *Our Catholic Heritage in Texas, 1519–1936*. Austin, TX: Von Boeckmann-Jones Company, 1936.

Chávez y Gilbert, Donald. *Origins of the First American Cowboys*. Cowboys–Vaqueros, NMHCPL.org.

Chipman, Donald E. *Spanish Texas, 1519–1821*. Austin: University of Texas Press, 1992.

Curtis, Edward S. *The North American Indian*. Vol. 17. Norwood, MA: The Plimpton Press, 1926.

David, W.W.H. *El Gringo*. Santa Fé, NM, 1938.

De Ágreda, María. *Mystical City of God*. Translated by Marison Fiscar. Washington, D.C.: AMI Press, 1971.

De Aragón, Ray John. "*El Conciliador: Resumen de la Vida del Padre Antonio José Martínez*." *El Hispano*, July 1975.

———. "*El Padre Martínez y el Obispo Lamy*." *La Luz Magazine*, April 1972.

———. "*El Santero de Mora*." *El Hispano*, June 1978.

———. *Enchanted Legends and Lore of New Mexico*. Charleston, SC: The History Press, 2012.

———. *Hermanos de la Luz/Brothers of the Light*. Santa Fé, NM: Heartsfire Books, 1998.

———. "*Mora Intrigue and Murder*." *New Mexico Magazine*, August 1982.

———. *Padre Martínez and Bishop Lamy*. Las Vegas, NM: Pan-American Publishing Co., 1976.

———. "*Padre Martínez Memory Scarred*." *El Hispano*, June 1978.

———. *Padre Martínez: New Perspectives from Taos*. Taos, NM: Millicent Rogers Museum, 1988.

———. "*Vida del Padre Antonio José Martínez*." *El Hispano*, July 1975.

Diario de Gobierno. *Plan of Tomé, October 19, 1837*. Santa Fé, NM: State Records Center and Archives, n.d.

Dublan, Manuel, and José María Lozano. *Constitutional Law of December 29, 1836; Legislacion mexicana o coleccion completa de las desposiciones legislativas expedidas desde la independencia de la republica*. Vol. 3. Mexico, 1876.

Duffus, R.L. *The Santa Fé Trail*. Albuquerque: University of New Mexico Press; Albuquerque, 1958.

Ellis, Richard N., ed. *New Mexico Historic Documents*. Albuquerque: University of New Mexico Press, 1975.

Espinosa, J. Manuel. *Crusaders of the Río Grande: The Story of Don Diego de Vargas and the Reconquest and Refounding of New Mexico*. Chicago: Institute of Jesuit History, 1942.

Ferrer, Joaquín María de. *Historia de la Monja Alférez (Doña Catalina de Erauso)*. Translation and annotations by Dan Harvey Pedrick. Madrid; Tipo Renovación, 1918.

Gregg, Josiah. *Commerce of the Praries*. Oklahoma, 1954.

Habig, Marion A. *O.F.M. Spanish Texas Pilgrimage: The Old Franciscan Missions and Other Spanish Settlements of Texas 1632-1821*. Chicago: Franciscan Herald Press, 1990.

Hammond, George P., and Agapito Rey. *Don Juan de Oñate, Colonizer of New Mexico, 1595–1628*. 2 vols. Albuquerque: University of New Mexico Press, 1953.

Hazen-Hammond. *A Short History of Santa Fé*. San Francisco: Lexikos, 1988.

Hickerson, Nancy Parrott. *The Jumanos: Hunters and Traders of the South Plains*. Austin: University of Texas Press, 1994.

Hodge, Frederick Webb, ed. *Handbook of American Indians North of Mexico*. 2 parts. Bureau of American Ethnology, Bulletin 30. Washington, D.C.: Government Printing Office, 1907–1910.

Hofman, Jack L. *Discovering Archaeology* 2, no. 1. (January/February 2000).

Jaramillo, Cleofas M. *Shadows of the Past/Sombras del Pasado, 1941*. Santa Fé, NM: Ancient City Press, 1972.

Kelly, Henry W. *Franciscan Missions of New Mexico, 1740–1760*. Albuquerque: Historical Society of New Mexico, 1941.

Kendrick, T.D. *Mary of Agreda: The Life and Legend of a Spanish Nun*. New York: Routledge & Kegan Paul, 1967.

Lecompte, Janet. *Rebellion in Rio Arriba*. Albuquerque: University of New Mexico Press, 1985.

Leonard, Irving A. *Baroque Times in Old Mexico: Seventeenth Century Persons, Places, and Practices*. Ann Arbor: University of Michigan Press, 1966.

Lewy, Guenter. "Were American Indians the Victims of Genocide?" History News Network, Seattle, WA, January 22, 2007.

Lowie, Robert H. *Indians of the Plains*. Garden City, NY: Natural History Press, 1962.

Lucero, Aurora. *Los Hispanos*. Denver, CO: Sage Books, 1947.

MacLeish, Archibald. *Conquistador*. Boston: Houghton Mifflin Co., 1932.

McSorley, Joseph. *An Outline History of the Church by Centuries*. St. Louis, MO: B. Herder Book Co., 1945.

Mexican Archives of New Mexico. Microfilm publication of the New Mexico State Records Center and Archives, Roll 24, Frame 807.

Nostrand, Richard L. *The Hispano Homeland*. Norman: University of Oklahoma Press, 1992.

Perrigo, Lynn I. *Hispanos-Historic Leaders in New Mexico*. Santa Fé, NM: Sunstone Press, 1985.

Prescott, William. *History of the Reign of Ferdinand and Isabella, The Catholic.* New York: J.B. Lippincott & Co., 1860.

Read, Benjamin. *Illustrated History of New Mexico*. Santa Fé: New Mexican Printing Co., 1912.

Reeve, Frank D. *History of New Mexico*. 2 vols. New York: Lewis Historical Publishing Co., 1961.

Rittenhouse, Jack D. *Disturnell's Treaty Map*. Santa Fé, NM: Stagecoach Press, 1965.

Simons, Helen, and Cathryn A. Hoyt, eds. *Hispanic Texas: A Historical Guide.* Austin: University of Texas Press, 1992.

Snell, Melissa. *The Spread of the Black Death through Europe.* About.com Guide, 2003.

Syers, William Edward. *Texas: The Beginning, 1519–1834*. Waco: Texian Press, 1978.

Twitchell, Ralph E. *The Military Occupation of New Mexico, 1846–1851*. Denver, CO: The Smith-Brooks Co., 1909.

Twitchell, Ralph E., ed. *Leading Facts of New Mexico History*. Vol. 2. Cedar Rapids, IA, 1912–17.

Tyler, Daniel. "Gringo View of Governor Armijo." *New Mexico Historical Review* 45 (January 1970).

Ulibarrí, Sabine. *Tierra Amarilla: Stories of New Mexico/Cuentos de Nuevo México*. Albuquerque: University of New Mexico, 1971.

Veles Giraldo, Juan R. *The Church in Spanish America and the Catholic Historical Review*. Anuario de Historia de la Iglesia 4. Pamplona: Universidad de Navarra, n.d.

Villagrá, Gaspar Pérez de. *Historia de la Nueva México, Alcalá, 1610*. Translated by Gilberto Espinosa. Los Angeles: Quivira Society, 1933.

Weber, David J., ed. *New Spain's Far Northern Frontier: Essays on Spain in the American West, 1540–1821*. Albuquerque: University of New Mexico Press, 1979.

About the Author

Ray John de Aragón is the author of *Enchanted Legends and Lore of New Mexico: Witches, Ghosts and Spirits*. He has appeared on many radio and television talk shows, including *De Colores* and *Illustrated Daily*. He has been featured in the *Albuquerque Journal*, the *New Mexican*, *El Hispano* and the *Tombstone Epitaph*. He has taught history at Luna Community College and the Valencia Branch of the University of New Mexico. He has done presentations on Spanish history at the Historical Society Conference held at the United World College of the American West, the Millicent Rogers Museum, the Harwood, the Museum of New Mexico and the Taos Historic Museums. He and his wife, Rosa María Calles, a noted playwright, were on the faculty of the 2011 Ninth Annual National Latino Writers Conference. Ray John has spent many years going off the beaten path, digging up the rich unwritten history, culture, traditions and heritage of New Mexico. His moving tales talk about the struggles, the hopes and the courage of an indomitable people.

www.ingramcontent.com/pod-product-compliance
Lightning Source LLC
LaVergne TN
LVHW052342100826
845147LV00021B/1151

* 9 7 8 1 6 0 9 4 9 7 6 0 6 *